CHRIST, THE CHURCH AND THE POOR

CHRIST, THE CHURCH AND THE POOR

Paul Gauthier

Translated by Edward Fitzgerald

THE NEWMAN PRESS
WESTMINSTER, MARYLAND
1965

CONTENTS

Author's Note

THE three chapters of this little book are presented in their logical order: the poor; the problem they present to the Church in Council; and one attempt at finding a response to the problem.

In fact, the three chapters were experienced in the reverse order: a cell of the Church was founded in Nazareth to win the poor to the Gospel: this was called the Companions of Jesus of Nazareth, the Carpenter, and is discussed in Part III. A proposed way of life for the Companions is set down in the Appendix. Then, the workers of Nazareth, encouraged by this apostolic brotherliness, wrote to the Fathers of the Council: the text of their appeal is to be found in Part II. Finally, it was felt to be necessary to describe and give the facts about this world of poverty, this ripening harvest, this flock without a shepherd, harassed and hungry, to a wider audience.

Soon we shall be able (and with what delight) to write about the reply made by the Fathers of the Council and recount how eagerly the reapers and the shepherds have come forward in reply to this appeal. But history must be made before it can be written.

Preface

I HAVE read Father Gauthier's book with great pleasure.
The very title—"Christ, the Church and the Poor"—
underlines a problem prominent in our hearts today. We
are delighted to see that the Vatican Council has raised it,
since this will doubtless ensure that it will henceforth be
given the prominent place it deserves in the hearts and
minds of all Christians.

One of the most serious reproaches advanced—even
though it arises from deceptive appearances—by those who
do not know the Church or at least do not know her real
teachings, is that she fails to attach to the problem of
poverty that primary importance its nature requires. Some
people even go so far as saying that the Church does not
seem to understand the problem fully. It is sufficient to
recall the true doctrine of which the Church is the guardian
to recognize the extent and gravity of such an error.

Father Gauthier's book is a further demonstration of this
truth. He is certainly entitled to claim that his book makes
the voice of the poor heard once more, and reminds us in
the spirit of the Bible of their sufferings and their hopes.

Whilst the Second Vatican Council was meeting in Rome,
a small group of bishops and priests came together from
time to time to discuss this question of poverty. The
exchanges that took place at these meetings not only gave
great joy to the participants, but also provided very useful

information on the problem. This little book by Father
Gauthier, who was one of the prime movers of these gatherings, is their echo, and for this we are all very grateful to
him.

Incidentally, are we likely to forget that on 11
September 1961 the Holy Father himself declared that the
Church presents herself to the world as she is and as she
desires to be: "the Church of all, but in particular the
Church of the poor"? And the Holy Father has repeated
the same thing on various occasions since.

I most sincerely hope that very many Christians will read
what Father Gauthier has to say in this book, and meditate
upon it. His words shed valuable light on the fundamental
problem of the relationship between the Church and
poverty.

Unfortunately the words of Father Chevrier, "the poor
are not yet won," are still true today. It is therefore more
than ever desirable that no one should be able to say with
truth that poor people do not feel at home in the Church.
Only the attitude of Christians themselves will one day
allow us to say in all truth that the poor do feel at home in
the Church. But I must point out that this will first require
great efforts on our part, and—to be quite frank—great
changes in the way many of us behave.

To say that this valuable little book will help many Christians to a true understanding of their duty in this respect
whilst at the same time inspiring them with the necessary
courage to do it manfully is a measure of the gratitude we
owe Father Gauthier for his work.

PIERRE MARIE, CARDINAL GERLIER
ARCHBISHOP OF LYONS

CHRIST, THE CHURCH AND THE POOR

I

THE POOR

Chapter One

The Poor

WORDS themselves seem to shy away from a too disturbing reality. In the face of death, for example, new words have been invented: decease, passing over, bereavement. Instead of saying "he is dead", many people say "he has passed away". Do words wear out, like coins? In using different words do people think they can soften a reality which is too cruel? Or perhaps reality itself changes its face? Something of the sort has happened with the words "poor" and "poverty". At one time "poor" was properly used to describe the starving, the shivering, the beggars, the proletarians. And "poverty" was the word used to describe their condition. Today we have to draw a distinction between poverty and destitution, between the poor and the truly wretched. People in drawing rooms and in well-meaning circles talk glibly of poverty without thinking over much of destitution. All Christians desire to be poor, but they forget the destitute. And this is nothing new.

You can see the same development in the Bible itself: at first poverty was regarded as a scandalous state of affairs, and one that ought not to exist at all in Israel. Later on sophisticated writings found that poverty was situated somewhere between opulence and destitution, and it became a synonym for humility and piety. However, the poor in spirit, the humble are usually simple people of modest condition. That's how it is in the Bible too. Jesus addressed them as "You, the poor . . . you that hunger" (Luke 6 : 20-21), and he declared that the poor in spirit were blessed (Matt. 5 : 3).

The spiritual and religious poverty that frees a man from material cares is indeed a blessing. It allows a man to possess goods and yet have a light heart, either because of a vow of poverty given within a community which takes care of the material needs of its members, or by personal or family property administered in obedience to the laws of the Church to the best of one's understanding and ability.

However, when what is involved is no longer merely a question of this spiritual conception of poverty but of real poverty in a far more definite and practical fashion, involving the real poor and their relationship to the Church, then the matter becomes very much more difficult. There is in particular a danger that consciences may be troubled, upset, and even wounded. And those who raise the question in the first place run the risk of being accused of communism, or marxism. In particular there is the ever-present danger of discussing harsh realities when it might in all humility be better to remain silent since mere words must seem vain, and only life itself, love and labour, can find a real approach to that world of anguish, hunger and misery.

And yet today the Church must strive to preach the Gospel to the poor as it was preached twenty centuries ago. In fact this is her primary mission and it derives from her own consecration, since the Church is Christ extended into our own day. Does not Jesus reveal that he has been "anointed" and sent "to preach good news to the poor"? (Luke 4 : 18).

Why is it so difficult to discuss the problem of the Church and the poor today? Some will assure us that it is because there aren't really any poor left—"only the workshys, you know". Others are even inclined to get angry and exclaim: "But it isn't the Church's job to provide mankind with bread; that is the business of governments and secular organizations." The mission of the Church is exclusively of a spiritual nature, they tell us, and to seek the bread of life literally would be to fall into the marxist trap. No, the mission of the Church is to seek the kingdom of God and his justice. They may even go on to say: "Incidentally, the rich are often spiritually poorer than the poor, and some seem rich who are, in fact, poor."

Such an attitude can be met with frequently amongst western Christians, and behind it you can sense a kind of defensive reaction, an excessive sensitivity. When you touch on the subject of the poor you are obviously touching a sore spot. In fact humanity is a body two-thirds covered with sore spots. It can be healed only in Christ, whom the Church extends into our own day. Outwardly, however, the Church would seem to be attached to the healthier part of humanity and have much less to do with the suffering and sorrows of the other two-thirds. But it is precisely this that inflicts a wound upon the body of Christ. Before considering this wound more closely and seeking to staunch it, let us first take a look at humanity itself.

Our immediate impression must be that it is torn into two: the rich on the one hand, the poor on the other. Of course, there is a whole pattern of variations in between, but ultimately it remains true that there are those who have more than they need in order to live, and those who do not even have enough. These things are relative, of course, and it isn't easy to define riches. Perhaps we may often consider the rich man as a child whose body has grown more rapidly than his soul (what he *has* is greater than what he *is*), whilst the poor man is like a child whose body is stunted but whose soul has grown (what he *has* is not sufficient for what he *is*). There is even some physical truth in this. Men tend to be bigger among rich people; amongst poor people they tend to be undersized. But feed a family of such undersized human beings properly for a generation or two and its off-spring will soon reach normal size.

Today it is no longer merely a question of rich individuals and poor individuals. Nowadays there are rich peoples and poor peoples, developed nations and under-developed nations. About a hundred years ago, proletarians became conscious of their unity. It is only about six years ago (at Bandung in 1957) that proletarian nations became conscious of theirs.

The Rich

It is quite true, of course, that even in this world—not to speak of the next—the rich are the real poor. Today's wealth is not so much money, or credits at the bank, as science, technology, political power, administrative position or even success on the screen. We are becoming a world of technocrats, and to some extent we have already got that far. Even so, the great ones of today, the scientists and the film stars, are not—unless they place their talents at the disposal of their brothers—those of whom the kingdom of heaven is made, since its mystery is "hidden from the wise and understanding" and revealed "to babes" (Luke 10:21). "God has scattered the proud, put down the mighty from their seats, and sent the rich empty away" (Luke 1:52-3). It was a poor and simple person, no other than Mary of Nazareth, who was privileged to announce that to the world.

Of course science, technology, politics—all these human activities—are necessary, but to be good they must be harnessed to the common weal and not exploited for personal gain. Though the technologists and the politicians may be the great ones of our day, it is still true that the biggest category of the rich consists of those who have money. Incidentally, technology and politics can both readily procure riches for their adepts—not all heads of States are like Ben Zvi, the Israeli President, who refused to allow his salary to be increased. Cinema stars sometimes accumulate millions and then die in loneliness, not knowing what to do either with their money or with themselves. Disgusted with life, Marilyn Monroe sought refuge in death. The Scandinavian countries are the most prosperous in Europe; they also have the highest suicide rate. The rich form a separate class, or rather separate classes, isolated from the rest of the world, and even from each other. The class war was not begun by working men, but by the rich as a result of their rivalries.

Some rich people have sufficient understanding to use their wealth for the common good, and in so doing they remain amongst the poor in spirit. One such, the possessor of one of the largest fortunes in the world, decided to use not only the income but also part of the capital to build working-class houses and children's homes, explaining: "My father amassed all this money by exploiting his workmen. I propose to make restitution." He also tried to win over other rich men to his noble idea, and to join with him in founding a loan bank to advance money to workmen and other poor people on long-term loans without security. After pursuing this idea for a number of years he finally had to face reality: "None of my rich friends will go along with me." This reminds us of an Arab proverb which says that the heart of a rich man is of stone.

Yet most rich men are really victims of their own wealth, since it alienates them from themselves. They seek in vain to compensate for the emptiness of their lives by making their fortunes still greater, seeking to find satisfaction in both business and pleasure. Their heart is truly where their treasure is: in a bank, a house, a piece of land, a factory, fine clothing. But everything is corrupted by egoism: "Your riches have rotted, and your garments are motheaten. . . .

Your gold and silver have rusted; and their rust ... will eat your flesh like fire" (James 5:2-3).

This is why the rich may truly be regarded as unfortunates here below, and yet still more so in the world to come. "Woe to you that are rich. ... Woe to you that are full. ... Woe to you that laugh now .... Woe to you, when all men speak well of you" (Luke 6:24-26). Jesus does not condemn, because he has not come to condemn but to save. He cries out in warning. The Greek word that Luke uses in this connection *ouaï* is as clear as its Hebrew equivalent *oï va voï*: your well-being is threatened! That threat is the evil of an empty heart in this world and the world to come. Perhaps its emptiness can be artificially disguised in this life, but not in the world to come, where it means damnation and absolute egoism.

Thus there can be no question of neglecting the rich. On the contrary, we must preach the Gospel to them too—the whole Gospel, in season and out of season. As we have seen, the Bible unquestionably contains very harsh words addressed to the rich, who must now hear them from the Church too. Not long ago a Jesuit Father declared: "If we had attached as much importance to the curses Christ addressed to the rich as we have to his proclamation 'Thou art Peter, and upon this rock I will build my Church', we should not have communism to contend with today." A Cardinal of the Curia to whom this remark was addressed smiled gently and beat his breast: "True, Father, true! But there is a difference. The 'Thou art Peter' passage does not upset anyone in the Church, and some people even think it to their advantage", and here the Cardinal pointed to himself. "But the curses Jesus addressed to the rich apply to us all, and thus they upset everyone."

The rich are entitled to hear the Gospel, particularly the commination of John the Baptist beginning: "You brood

of vipers. Who warned you to flee from the wrath to come?"
And again: "He who has two coats, let him share with him
who has none; and he who has food, let him do likewise"
(Luke 3:7, 11).

The rich are entitled to be warned that they will be
judged according to the bread, the clothing and the love
they have given to the living Jesus in his suffering
members: "Depart from me you cursed, into eternal
fire.... For I was hungry, and ye gave me no food"
(Matt. 15:41-2).

In our day the United States of America possesses and
consumes 40 per cent of this world's material goods, though
its population amounts to only 6.7 per cent of the world
total. In the Far East, on the other hand, 52.3 per cent of
the total population of the world possesses and consumes
only 12.3 per cent of the world's goods.

It is quite true that rich countries are now assisting poor
ones, but they are doing it in somewhat the same way that
individual rich assist the poor. Their aid is still reminiscent
of the lines in which a Spanish poet celebrated a hospital
built by a very rich man named Don Juan de Porrés:

> "The Senor Don Juan de Porrés,
> Of charity beyond compare,
> Built the hospital that here stands,
> Since he so loved the meek and poor
> —though first of all he made them poor."

Isn't it high time for us to urge those rich people who
call themselves Christians: "Do penance and believe in the
Gospel!"?

Of course, the meaning of the Gospel is not exhausted
in the sharing out of this world's goods, but poverty is the
sign of Jesus of Nazareth, the Word made flesh, "who is

dead and is yet alive". Jesus lives in just the same way in
those of his members who are hungry. The Gospel is the
search for the kingdom of God and its justice; but its holy
justice begins with justice pure and simple, both distri-
butive and social. The Gospel is the affirmation of God, the
God who is, and the God who is love. "But if any
one has the world's goods, and sees his brother in need,
yet closes his heart against him, how does God's love abide
in him?" (I John 3:17). "What does it profit, my brethren,
if a man says he has faith, but has not works? Can his faith
save him? If a brother or sister is ill-clad, and in lack of daily
food, and one of you say to them: "Go in peace, be warmed
and filled" without giving them the things needed for the
body, what does it profit?" (James 2:14).

The Illiterate

In our modern world to give a man what he needs for
his body means to give him the opportunity of earning his
living, including, of course, that instruction and training
that will permit him to stay abreast of technological
developments. Now despite all our progress there are still
a great number of illiterates in the world. There are no very
accurate figures available on the question, but it has been
estimated that about a third of the world's population can
neither read nor write. For example, one Brazilian bishop
reports that no less than 40 per cent of his flock are
illiterates. In Africa, thanks to modern transistor radios,
the wireless penetrates into the villages before the school
does, and takes the place of the oral instruction previously
given at the end of the day by the father of the family in
the village square.

It is difficult for those who can read and write to imagine
the poverty of illiterates. It is a poverty that affects the
very spirit itself. Unquestionably it is also quite com-

patible with profound wisdom and great saintliness. But such poverty strangely reduces the dimensions of the world, and is a source of contempt and often misery.

At Nazareth, as in many of the countries in the Near East, the Levant, the Orient, Africa and Latin America, the watershed lies between the generation born forty years ago or so, when the majority of working men and poor people were condemned to illiteracy, and those who were born only ten years or so ago and now get free schooling. Abou Said (the father of Said) cannot sign his name and must suffer the humiliation of giving his finger-print instead of his signature. But his son Said goes to school and will stay there until he is at least fourteen.

The educated man will retain that interior wealth represented by culture even when he is deprived of everything else. Thanks to his knowledge he can arrive at possessions, power and fortune. If he is called to religious poverty, he does not fail to retain (and even often develop) that inner wealth which comes from the spirit. This too is compatible with saintliness, and there have been saints whose intellectual labours have borne fruit for the kingdom of heaven. Theology is a science, even the king of sciences. But there have also been saints who could neither read nor write. Bernadette Soubirous was an illiterate little shepherdess when the Immaculate chose her as her confidant. And Mary the Immaculate of Nazareth herself probably didn't know her letters any better than the other women of her people in those days. And of Jesus himself they said : "He has not studied." The Scribes, the Doctors and the Pharisees were scornful of the simple people who did believe in him. The rabble "who do not know the law are accursed. . . . No prophet is to rise from Galilee" (John 7 : 49, 52). Jesus was only a Galilean and he wrote in the sand with his finger. His wisdom was of a different order, that of charity, his own kind of wisdom. "And though . . . I understand all mysteries and knowledge . . . and have not love I am nothing" (I Cor. 13 : 2).

The Starvelings

In a single year in the United States they spend forty million dollars on slimming pills. It is not unreasonable to suppose that at least three times that sum was spent on the excessive eating that made the slimming pills necessary. But two-thirds of the population of the world are under-nourished and live in a permanent state of semi-famine. What should we think of a village in which, say, forty of a total number of 120 inhabitants ate their fill, and more than their fill, whilst the remaining eighty went hungry? Yet this is the situation with regard to humanity as a whole. In the great human family the sons of men in the greater part of the Near and the Far East have not enough to eat. The same is true of the population of Bolivia. In South America the people of the Argentine and of Uruguay are only a little better off than their indigent neighbours. The people of Latin America just about get by. In Darkest Africa the people often do not have enough to eat. In the Sahara men have only a handful of dates for their daily nourishment, and are glad to get them. In the Near East it is a few olives and a morsel of bread. In India it is a bowl of rice. Many families in Trivandrum in the south of India have about fifty dollars a year on which to live.

In Africa, India, Latin America and other parts of the world a disease known under various names emaciates the children, saddening their faces and swelling their bellies. The scientists call it farinaceous atrophy, nutritional atrophy, infantile atrophy, and so on. The reality is much simpler; it's just hunger; lack of food; lack of proteins.

Carolina Maria de Jésus notes in her diary for 15 June : [1] "I stopped at a newstand. I read that a woman with three children had committed suicide because she found it too difficult to live. The poor woman! What a shame against a nation. A person who kills herself because of hunger. The worst thing that a mother can hear is the symphony: 'Mama, I want some bread! Mama, I'm hungry!' I spent the whole day cursing the politicians because I, as well, when I don t have anything to give to my children, almost go crazy."

Three years ago in Nazareth, Jiries, a Christian Arab workman, really did go out of his mind because he could not earn enough to feed his six children. "It drives me out of my mind that I can't give my children enough to eat," he exclaimed. And near the famous fountain of the Virgin pilgrims watched a little girl raking through a dustbin to fill her small bag with discarded food refuse. "She's an orphan, and she's getting food for her little brothers," explained the local guide apologetically, whilst the tourists looked on in embarrassment that such things could be in the village of Mary and Jesus.

There are people who commit suicide because they have not enough to eat, but many more die of slow malnutrition. Every year in the Sahara scores of the sons of God die in this way, and no one talks of famine. In certain drought years many thousands die, and there is no greater stir. In India a religious has founded a hospital to collect those who would otherwise die of starvation on the streets. They then die of starvation in the hospital, of course, but at least they are under a roof and they can die quietly, piously and un-observed. There is a friendly hand to close their eyes for the last time, and there is a good soul to love them as fellow human beings, and pray with them a little before they die.

What is the cause of this world-wide endemic famine?

[1] *Child of the Dark* (New American Library, New York, 1963), p. 60.

It is not, as might be thought, due to any world-wide lack of the food humanity requires for its sustenance; it is due solely to the maldistribution of this food. The excessive exploitation of nature by man in certain places also plays a role but it is above all due to the exploitation of man by man. How often can you pick up a newspaper and find your eye attracted by a headline which informs you that there has been such a bumper harvest of, say, wheat that the farmers don't know what to do with it all. And in the same newspaper you may well see another headline which asks: "Can the world feed its growing number of inhabitants?"

There are many people who throughout their whole lives never know what it is to eat their fill. The blood that runs sluggishly through their veins is not rich like yours. They live with empty bellies, or bellies swollen from food of such poor quality that it impoverishes their blood and makes them listless. Their haggard eyes are jaundiced; for them the world is yellow—the colour of famine.

When Jesus comes again and says: "I was hungry and you fed me not," he will be saying that he suffered hunger in our day in many of his members, and we shall be judged accordingly.

The Ragged and the Homeless

And the Judge will also say: "I was naked. . . . I was homeless." After food, it is clothing of which the poor are chiefly deprived; and after clothing, lodging—the great clothing of a roof over one's head. Those who have always had a good home and a change of clothing can hardly realize what it means for a man to have only one garment, and that worn and tattered, which he cannot change because he has no other; or to live in a mean shanty made perhaps of wood or corrugated iron, or perhaps a chicken-house or pigsty, or even just a hole in the ground. There

are many, many people in India who have not even this;
they live all their lives, day and night, on the streets, and
it is there they finally die.

Housing exercises a great influence on a man's life. A
family which is forced to live in a slum suffers physical and
moral degeneration but, once re-housed, it will rise up the
social and economic scale in the course of a single year.

Unfortunately there are still very many places where
such re-housing still remains to be done. Not so long ago
it was calculated that even in France something like
five million people were still inadequately housed, i.e. no
less than 22 per cent of the population of the big towns.
But the lowest depths of housing misery in the West is
probably reached in the so-called "Favellas", the slum
dwellings in the suburbs of big towns like Sao Paulo in
Brazil. Details of this wretchedness have recently been
published. In note-books themselves picked out of dust-
bins, Carolina Maria de Jésus records not only her own
hunger and that of her children, but the hunger of all those
wretched day labourers and theirs. "The favella is the cess-
pool of the city," she writes. "Both men and rubbish are
tipped there, and the two mingle. Everything the city no
longer wants is thrown here." Sometimes the miserable
hovels of the poor are right in the heart of great cities, like
Trastevere in Rome, where many hundreds of impoverish-
ed families live huddled together around the palace of a
bachelor prince, men, women and children in a decaying
and unhealthy quarter.

When the Eucharistic Congress in Rio de Janeiro was
over, Cardinal Gerlier took one of the Brazilian bishops to
one side and said: "Tell me frankly as man to man: do you
really think we can afford such ostentation in a city surrounded by such wretchedness?" From that day the bishop
devoted himself to alleviating poverty, and in particular he
set out to provide the Lord with decent lodgings: "I was

a stranger and you welcomed me; naked and you clothed me" (Matt. 25:35-36). Was it in foreknowledge that he would live with his homeless members that Christ desired to suffer outside the city, outside the gate, that he was born in a stable outside Bethlehem "because there was no room for them in the inn"?

The Sick

Badly fed, badly clothed and badly lodged, human beings deprived of their elementary needs, food, clothing and a sound roof over their heads, are very vulnerable to sickness. A sick man is in poor physical condition, and very often spiritually distressed as well. An old invalid in the small and dilapidated hospital of St John of Acre in Galilee said sadly: "I am alone in the world." A man's body is normally the instrument of communication and communion with his like. But if his body is sick, broken and disfigured, how should he communicate with the outside world and with his fellow sons of men? Who is anxious to kiss a leper? The sick demand no more than a visit. "I was sick and you visited me," the judge will say. "Sick or in prison" (Matt. 25:36, 44). On the day of judgement the sick and the prisoner will be together, for sickness is a prison; it cuts off a man from the society of the rich in health.

The world of the sick is vast. There are no less than two million lepers vegetating on this planet at this very moment, one to every 1,500 human beings; one leper in every small town of 1,500 inhabitants; 100 lepers in a town of 150,000 inhabitants. The very word "leper" is frightening, and very few ordinary, healthy people know what a leper looks like. Those lepers who have friends to look after them are fortunate indeed, men like Father Damien, women like the White Sisters and the Little Sisters of the Poor. But how many others are there who have no one to look after them? They are excluded from the cities and warded off like dangerous beasts. And nevertheless often they are sufferers whose souls have been refined by their suffering, whose souls are strangely beautiful in hideous bodies.

One such is Ibrahim, a muslim, a patient in the little leper colony of Siloam in the valley of Cedron near Jerusalem. His feet, one hand and part of his face have been eaten away by leprosy. When he is visited by Christians who are there on a pilgrimage he sings Christian hymns to them in Arabic and reads them passages from the Koran about the immaculate Virgin. Hearing on one occasion that some of them came from Nazareth in Israel he asked them to take a message of peace and fraternity to the Jews of Israel. Now this man lost everything, including his health, as a result of the war between the Arabs and the Jews in 1948. When the hour of prayer sounds he drags himself to the window and shouts out into the valley of Cedron: "God is God...."

At least leprosy does not attack the soul; alcoholism is a worse form of leprosy because it corrupts the human spirit. Itself the product of misery, bad housing, unemployment and boredom, in its turn it produces nothing but misery. Alcoholism is widespread even in districts where the people are not poor, as for example in Normandy and Brittany. But very often those who drink to excess are those who are seeking to forget their misery, moral or physical. Physically exhausted, man seeks stimulation in alcohol, which is a kind of nourishment. Half a litre of cheap red wine costs less than a sandwich, and produces an immediate sensation of comfort and consolation. Alcohol corrodes the physical organism, undermines morality, and destroys the home. In France in 1956 a quarter of the population were alcoholics, 25 per cent, on an average 250 alcoholics in a village of 1,000 inhabitants!

Medical treatment or economic assistance, both of which

do not touch the heart of man, are not the only remedies —as, indeed, they are not in many other cases of misery. If, for example, an alcoholic is to be saved then, in addition to medical treatment, he needs the fraternity of companions who will look after him and forswear alcohol with him. Voluntary abstainers group together in this way and are instrumental in saving alcoholics by pledging themselves never to touch alcohol. Hundreds of families have been saved from ruin by the activities of such fraternities. There is an outstandingly important lesson for us here : you can save a man only by living his life with him, and not merely by doing something to him.

To save mankind Jesus desired to realize the prophecy of Isaiah in himself, and in his Passion to become the Servant of Yahveh; he of whom it was said : "His appearance was so marred beyond human resemblance . . . and his form beyond that of the sons of men. . . . He was despised and rejected by men; a man of sorrows and acquainted with grief; and as one from whom men hide their faces he was despised, and we esteemed him not. Surely he has borne our griefs and carried our sorrows. . . . But he was wounded for our transgressions, he was bruised for our iniquities . . . like a lamb that is led to the slaughter" (Is. 52 : 14; 53 : 2-4, 5, 7).

This appears so very true in the case of the sick and of those who have been maimed at their work. How many working men are old and worn out before their time because they are the victims of inhuman conditions of labour? Yet they have no alternative, since they must earn bread for themselves and their families where they can, whilst at the same time enriching those for whom they are forced to labour. This sort of thing is still not uncommon, particularly in the mining areas. In Charleroi there are hundreds of miners who after twenty years in the mines, and sometimes even less, are suffering from pulmonary disease. If they have worked the necessary number of years in the mines they receive a small pension. Ultimately they die from a kind of asthma, choking and in great pain. A Spanish workman named Pablo left his own country to find work in the Belgian mines. In time he contracted this terrible disease, and in a brain storm threatened to hurl his wife and children, whom he most certainly loved, out of the window. "Kill me," he begged. "Kill me before I kill my wife and children." If every sick man undergoes in his own body the Passion of Christ, how much more then do those who share with him the burden of this world's sins and are themselves the victims of man's exploitation by man?

The Despised and Rejected

Sickness merely attacks and exhausts the body, and some sick people manage to retain an astonishing spiritual strength. The leper Ibrahim is an example. Contempt does not deprive a man of his bodily health and strength, or of his food and clothing, but it does deprive him of that human atmosphere which is perhaps even more necessary to life —the esteem, the respect, the integrity and the dignity of his person.

The Beatitudes tell us that in the last resort the poor man is he who is despised. "Blessed are you poor. . . . Blessed are you when men hate you, and when they exclude you, and revile you, and cast out your name as evil, on account of the Son of man" (Luke 6 : 20, 22).

In the same way it is for the Son of man's sake, coupled unknowingly with the derision of "Ecce Homo" and the scourging, that the deported, the displaced persons, the prisoners, those races which are condemned as inferior, the Jews, and so many women and so many children suffer. They suffer the contempt of the powerful, and they are mocked by those who think themselves superior because they are the lords of the world.

Is it not a special form of human contempt when hundreds of thousands of people are driven from their homes and out of their own countries as innocent victims of the policy of the great and the powerful? In Jordan and in Syria and in the Gaza pocket there are some 800,000 souls waiting under canvas and in small huts with nothing to do. They are parked in great camps like so much merchandise waiting to be bartered in the diplomatic market, where they serve as the stakes. And even worse than these camps are the prisons where men lie awaiting the judgement of their fellow men. "I was in prison, and you came to me" (Matt. 25:36). How many of these wretched men never know even that short moment of liberty when they see a beloved face, receive a familiar smile, and hear a kindly human word? Deprived of their liberty, those who are detained in concentration camps soon become deprived of their morale too. Crowded together like beasts, frequently condemned to forced labour, they risk losing their personality at the eleventh hour. Brain-washing effaces all trace of liberty. "Behold the man!" Pilate washed his hands; today, it is the thoughts of the accused which are washed.

It is only comparatively recently that Negroes and other such peoples have been recognized as human beings at all, and this is not true everywhere even now. Burdened by centuries of contempt, the songs they sing to keep in good heart record their sufferings and their long wait for justice: "One more river to cross," "We shall overcome." How much longer must they still suffer racial discrimination in Rhodesia and California and elsewhere? But right down to our own times the most despised and the most persecuted of all the sons of men are undoubtedly the Jews. And how has it come about that Christians should have played a leading part in this terrible persecution of the Jews, when their own Lord and Master is himself a Jew? Can it be that they have never read the epistle of Paul to the Romans, chapters 9, 10, and 11? "For I could wish that I myself were accursed and cut off from Christ for the sake of my brethren. . . . They are Israelites, and to them belong the sonship, the glory, the covenants, the giving of the law, the worship, and the promises; to them belong the patriarchs, and of their race according to the flesh, is the Christ. . . . For if their rejection means the reconciliation of the world, what will their acceptance mean but life from the dead. . . . And so all Israel will be saved" (I Rom. 9 : 3-4; 11 : 15, 26).

In Belgium under the Nazi occupation a little Jewish girl escaped during a raid in which her parents were seized and deported. She was hidden on a farm by Christians who gave her soup and bread, but did so saying, "There, dirty little Jewess, eat". And this she heard every day for four years. For centuries her kind have heard this same sort of thing : "race accursed, deicides, dirty Jews!" And it was not until the days of Hitler and Eichmann that the consciences of honest men were aroused at last. "Can the Jews forget that they are dispersed amongst peoples, who did nothing to stand between them and destruction; amongst innumerable beings, who, with a few courageous exceptions, either assisted in their destruction or stood indifferently aside."[1] How could Christians fail to see a sign set up over these millions of beloved sons of God, a sign written in three languages, Latin, Greek and Hebrew, "Jesus of Nazareth, King of the Jews". "Hands off the Jews!" cries Bernard with the authentic voice of the Church. "Since the Jews are the flesh and bones of our Lord."

Far from being an accursed race they remain a chosen race because "the election of God knoweth no repentance". The few Jews who condemned and crucified Jesus in the

[1] Haim Gouri, "Face à la cage de verre".

2

Passion under the Roman Pontius Pilate were merely, alas, instruments of human sin. They thought to pay special devotion to God by showing contempt for the man Jesus who claimed to be God. The rejection of God begins and ends always in contempt for man. The time of contempt for God is always a time of contempt for man, and, conversely, contempt for man is contempt for God.

Women and Children

When whole races are despised as inferior it is always on the basis of some pseudo-philosophic or religious argument, but contempt for women and children is altogether gratuitous: absolute contempt for the poor, contempt for the weak. Aristotle even denied that a woman has a soul at all. And even in our own day, how many places are there where the woman is either a female animal in luxury or a beast of burden?

In *The Second Sex* Simone de Beauvoir describes her attempts to analyse this scandal. How did the mind of the man, the strong one, work to make him think he could afford to despise his wife and his mother in this way?

Many thousands of women live in the worst form of contempt, the worst form of misery, the most infamous form of slavery, that of prostitution. Millions of other women are still slaves of social structures in which man apes the Lord of Creation. Even in monogamous marriages there are only too many men who allow their supposed superiority to weigh heavily on their wives.

The profanation of human love is a particularly serious fall from grace because human love is the noblest reflection of the love of God. The Song of Songs uses the one to praise the other, as Osee presents the fidelity of God by comparison with that of married couples.

"Woman, what have you to do with me," said Jesus.

"Woman, behold thy son!" Is a woman not Mother of God for ever? The Gospel has nothing but indulgence for women, and pardon for the sinner, the adultress. To Mary Magdalene whom he delivered of seven demons (no doubt the harlot of whom St Luke speaks) Jesus said: "Go and tell my brethren" (Matt. 28:10). It is time to listen to what this woman has to say to us, the woman who was the first witness of the resurrection of the Son of Man, born of woman.

Even in the natural order, woman is a revelation of the tenderness of God for man, as man represents the hope of salvation for woman. In marriage the man is the image of Christ the Saviour for the woman, and the woman is the image of the grace of Christ in his Church for the man. The gift of herself that the woman makes to the man can be a revelation of God, salvation through the flesh itself, the prelude to the Resurrection. And even in sin, when the man profanes the temple of the spirit, more than one man who sought nothing but base pleasure to be paid for in cash discovered a vision of God in the purity of soul of the woman he thought just a prostitute. The story Knut Ledin tells in "Les Larmes de Dieu" is neither imaginary nor unique. Whilst embracing the body of the woman delivered to prostitution by misery or social pressure, the man becomes aware that "inside her heart is the incorruptibility of a calm and serene soul". The most profound understanding of the soul of woman is that of St Peter, who was himself a married man, and who wrote: "Likewise you husbands, live considerately with your wives, bestowing honour on the woman as the weaker sex, since you are joint heirs of the grace of life" (I Peter 3:7). The most frequent cause of prostitution is moral and material misery. Those who have neither enough to eat and drink, nor the means wherewith to clothe themselves or to provide a roof over their heads; those whose hearts are empty of all affection

and who lack guidance; those who have children to feed,
sometimes even children born as the result of their wretched
profession—such people become almost of necessity the
victims of this exploitation by man. This exploitation is,
incidentally, very profitable for those who organize it and
take for themselves the greater part of the profit, leaving
the women only just enough to live on. In 1939 in France
the so-called *maisons de tolérance*, or officially licensed
brothels, had a business turn-over of a milliard francs. These
houses have since been closed down but the sexual exploitation of women continues. There is, for example, still a
White Slave traffic which provides women for the harems
of Arabia and elsewhere.

Like women, children have been—and still remain in
many countries and many places—an object of gratuitous
and absolute contempt purely on account of their weakness
and poverty. Not so long ago an unwanted child in China
—particularly if it were a girl—was thrown onto the
midden, or left in the street. And it is also not so very long
ago that Vincent de Paul had to fight in his country to
secure recognition for the fact that a child is never the fruit
of sin, and that it always has a right to life. Is a child not
the fruit of love, which in complete intimacy should always
be a mutual and full gift in the hope of a life born of that
communion at the source of all life, which is called
love?

Once a child is born and normal, this right is not disputed
nowadays. But if the child is not normal, or is simply conceived in the womb of its mother, this right is still often
denied. Poor and weak, the child is completely dependent.
It can only hope to be loved. Perhaps that is why, when
wishing to reveal himself to men, the eternal God, creator
of the cosmos, desired first of all to be conceived in the womb
of a woman in order to be love alone. At Nazareth there is
a painting in the Orthodox Church of the Assumption by

an early artist who has not hesitated to place a small child with a golden halo in the womb of the Virgin Mary. "The Word made Flesh," the germ of life, eternal life.

No sooner was he born, than this child was threatened and had to be hurried off like a displaced person and carried into Egypt, a country in which his people had once known slavery. In the absence of this one child Herod massacred all the remaining children below the age of two years. The Church now honours and remembers them as the Holy Innocents. But what about the millions of innocents who are still massacred at birth, sometimes indeed even before they are born at all, because they have absolutely nothing in this world, not even the loving heart of a mother. All they are is creatures made in the image of he who is, absolutely poor in possessions, altogether rich in being.

Quite certainly the most usual reason for being despised in this world is to have nothing. Those who possess this world's goods, on the other hand, are looked up to for their power and their fortune.

What is a man worth who possesses little or nothing? In many well-to-do countries the question of a man's worth is invariably taken to refer to his bank balance. In the same way the peoples despised as inferior are those which are poor and under-developed. Whilst the Jews were dispersed amongst the peoples and segregated in their ghettos they were also despised and massacred. Those of them who were rich and occupied powerful positions in society were not less despised, but they had much less to fear. They provoked anger, but it fell on their poorer brethren who had nothing. Now that the Jews have returned to their own country and made themselves into a strong nation, well equipped and well armed, they are given consideration and respect. Not so long ago a slogan was scrawled on the Métro walls in Paris: "Long live Israel! Down with the Jews!"

The Working People

It is true that this despised Jewish people has now succeeded—in the words of the philosopher David Gordon,
who became a labourer in the marshlands to the south of
Lake Genesareth in the Degania Kibbutz—"in accomplish-
ing the redemption of man and of the earth by labour".
Theologically speaking, of course, what David Gordon says
is not altogether accurate, but it is a part of the truth. Hard
labour and working-class organization have brought about
the resurrection of Israel, a land which was thought
capable of sustaining perhaps half a million inhabitants,
but which today sustains around three million souls, whilst
its milk and egg production even shows a surplus. By hard
labour the pioneers of Israel have drained the marshes of
Jordan and turned them into fertile valleys and fields where
bananas and other fruits grow. They have dug the hills of
Judea and made orchards and vineyards there. They have
irrigated the Negev desert, which is now producing wheat.
Altogether modern Israel is a wonderful example of what
man by his labour can make a barren land do for him.

Man redeems himself by labour, by the command of the
Creator: "In the sweat of your face you shall eat bread"
(Gen. 3 : 19). This is not a negative punishment; it is already
participation in the Redemption, because the seed of the
woman shall bruise the head of the serpent (Gen. 3 : 15).
The Redeemer himself decided to labour as a carpenter
in order to save humanity. For man, to labour is to take
part in his own Redemption, in time and in eternity, on
earth and in heaven, materially and spiritually. The two
orders are certainly distinct, and there is a marxist atheist
interpretation of labour which is a mere caricature of the
true redemption. But there is also a Christian interpretation
of labour which redeems in the name of Christ. Though
the two orders are distinct they are not separate. On the

terrestrial, temporal and material plane man can free himself from want. Even in work man can reach a certain fulfilment. Not only does labour permit a man to earn his bread, it also allows him to become more of a man, to share human solidarity and take his part in the construction of the terrestrial city. This has been made very clear in respect of the Jews. They were despised as lazy and parasitic, though, in fact, manual labour was forbidden to them in most countries. This prohibition deformed them both physically and psychologically. But nowadays in labouring on their own soil they have taken on a new personality, and become a new type both morally and physically.

On the spiritual, eternal and celestial plan labour allows man to co-operate with the Creator, who has charged him to go forth and dominate the earth, take possession of it, and complete the creation. Labour allows a man to save himself from sin by offering up the fatigue and pain of labour. Labour allows man to commune with the carpenter of Nazareth and through him with all his brothers, and with the Father himself, who "labours unceasingly", and with the creative spirit. All this is splendid.

How has it come about that labour has become one of the most frequent and one of the most serious occasions of the exploitation of man by man, and of human degeneration? That exploitation of man, the image of God, by another in the same image, which now degenerates into a satanic caricature, is no new phenomenon. Once it was called by the name of slavery. Then it became serfdom. Now it is the wage system.

Wage labour can be just, of course, provided it is regulated by the labour and social contract. In some countries wage workers have attained a very acceptable status, but then there are invariably strong trade unions to defend their rights. And if they are organized in co-operatives then there is no longer anything in common between their lot

and that of a proletariat. In climbing up the social ladder
these workmen left behind everything which once
associated them with the proletariat. Unfortunately, working men who have achieved this relatively secure and
favourable standard of living, with good housing, a refri-
gerator, television, and perhaps a car, may be inclined to
forget their comrades who are not so well off. Their hearts
and their consciences both tend to harden as they rise to
a place amongst the well-to-do in our present world.

However, in many countries, and in the most thickly
populated at that, the proletariat is still in the majority.
Where working men are not strongly organized they are
at the mercy of those who employ them: "Get on with the
job first and then we'll see how much you're worth," is the
sort of thing working men hear only too often when they
present themselves at the factory gate or on the site and
ask for work. For a hard day's work in such circumstances
a man will just about earn enough to keep himself from
actually starving. And that is how it was not so very long
ago in both France and England. The song of the silk
weavers of Lyons, the so-called Canutes, is a moving testi-
mony to the first awakening of working men to a realization
of the social injustices which prevailed in the middle of the
nineteenth century:

"Pour chanter Véni Creator
Il faut avoir chasuble d'or.
Nous en tissons pour vous gens d'Eglise.
Et nous pauvres canuts n'avons pas de chemise.
C'est nous les canuts et nous allons tous nus (rep.)

Pour gouverner il faut avoir
Manteaux et rubans en sautoir
Nous entissons pour vous grands de la terre
Et nous pauvres canuts sans drap on nous enterre.

C'est nous les canuts et nous allons tous nus (rep.)

Mais notre règne arrivera
Quand votre règne finira

Nous tisserons alors le linceul du vieux monde
Car on entend déja la tempête qui gronde.

C'est nous les canuts et vous irez tous nus (rep.)[1]

A hundred years later the same plaints can be heard in lands that call themselves Christian. Last Christmas a working woman with sixteen years in the factory behind her wrote: "We are forced down in the factory, why should we go on our knees in the church? The factory means nothing to us, neither does the church. We understand nothing in the factory, and we understand nothing in church. Yes, of course, there are differences, but that's how it really is. In the meantime we suffer together with the defeated Christ, in joy, in his joy, that of the despised and rejected who is nevertheless the Son of God."

[1] To sing the Veni Creator
You need chasubles of gold
We weave them for you, Churchmen
Yet we poor weavers lack even shirts.

We are the weavers, yet we go bare. (*Repeat*).

To govern us you need purple cloaks
And ribbons and orders.
We weave them for the great ones of this earth.
But they bury us poor weavers without winding sheets.

We are the weavers, yet we go bare. (*Repeat*).

But our time will come
When your time is over
We'll weave the winding sheet of this old world
Hear the thunder of the approaching storm!

We are the weavers, but then you will go bare. (*Repeat*).

That working woman has retained her faith. But how many have lost it, or never received it at all, on account of a scandalous situation that marxism finds it so easy to exploit?

In his *Capital*, Karl Marx writes of "the lumpen or slum proletariat ... the demoralized and degenerate, the unemployable ... persons who outlive the normal age of a worker; and finally, the victims of industry (whose number continually grows with the spread of dangerous machinery, the increase in the mining industry, the growth of chemical factories, etc.).... Pauperism constitutes the infirmary of the active labour army.... Finally, the larger the Lazarus stratum of the working class, and the larger the industrial reserve army, the larger, too, is the army of those who are officially accounted paupers."[1] This description retains its accuracy for whole regions in Bolivia, Jordan and India. As Pius XI said in *Quadragesimo Anno*, "Material emerges from the factory refined; the workman is degraded".

The first social laws forbade the employment of children under the age of ten in factories, and the employment of women below the age of eighteen on night work in the blast furnaces. Such laws are less than a hundred years old in Europe, and in some countries they still do not exist. As late as 1949 naked children were working in Chinese coal mines. They were known as "ants", because they were so small that they could crawl into places in the mines were adults could not go. What is the situation in this respect in 1963?

Spanish, Italian and Greek working men are still being drawn to the mines in Belgium today in the hope of earning their living, but fifteen years of such underground labour can lead to the illness and suffering we have already mentioned.

[1] Karl Marx, *Capital*, Vol. II., J. M. Dent, "Everyman" edition, London 1930, pp. 711-2.

This so-called world of labour is far from being baptized or won. In the one case labour without social organization remains the exploitation of man by man and causes him to lose his soul. In the other case the social organization and the mystique of labour and technique leads the workman and the technician to forget this soul. It is, of course, by labour and social organization that humanity is able to gain its daily bread and the clothing of which it stands in need, but the world of labour and even that of socialization have not yet received the light of Christ. Yet Jesus became a carpenter and identified himself with the workers of the world. Leo XIII, Pius XI, and, latterly, John XXIII in his encyclical *Mater et Magistra*, have laid down the basis for a sound and healthy doctrine of labour and socialization. Nevertheless, this world of labour stands far from the Church.

When you come across certain things in your reading you can well understand why the working masses distrust the Church. "We must protect religion because it teaches the people right morals, and in particular that they are born to suffer." This is the pseudo-Christian Taine writing in all seriousness and without irony. Karl Marx and the others have had things made too easy for them in this way : "The social principles of Christianity explain all the infamies which the oppressed suffer at the hands of their oppressors either as a just punishment for original sin, or as trials imposed on the elect by the Lord in his wisdom." This, of course, is quite wrong both according to the Bible and according to the Church, but—alas!—it is only too often accepted and practised by certain profiteers of Christianity. The result is that the working man remains without God and without hope in his own world. Unless they receive the Gospel at the hands of the Church, humanity seeks gropingly for hope and only too often falls victim to marxism.

An inquiry conducted in 1952 in the Charleroi neighbourhood, which is supposed to be Christian, showed that
only about 3 per cent of all working men went to church.
Similarly, in Brazil, in a diocese of 300,000 inhabitants, there
are only three diocesan priests, and the working men
employed in the great sugar industry of the neighbourhood
(several of the factories have more than 15,000 employees)
are completely outside the influence of the Church.

Those Without God and Without Hope

The working people are not alone in being generally
speaking without God and without hope. The same applies
to many intellectuals, who do not see the Saviour in the
Church. They feel that the Church shows no interest in
their problems, and God himself seems absent.

A Jew who had survived incarceration in a concentration
camp found himself unable to pray because he had
experienced and witnessed so many terrible things: thousands of innocent children herded into the gas chambers
and crematoria. "Praying seemed to me blasphemous."

Humanity becomes conscious of itself only to find itself
after a long past of pain and suffering in a state which is
still wretched. The majority of its members suffer from
hunger, privation and injustice. Growth does nothing but
accentuate this wretchedness. What is the explanation of
this and how can it be remedied? How could a world which
calls itself Christian have allowed such a situation to come
about?

In face of such chaos some people feel that everything is
pointless. Many atheist existentialists, and many people are
that without consciously knowing anything of this erudite
philosophy, are scandalized at the evil there is in this world.
"If there were a God," they say, "and if he were good, then
he would be unable to tolerate such misery for human

beings". Or : "If God were good he would have created man good. But men are bad. Therefore God can't be good, and he doesn't exist anyway." This is the popular form of this atheism of despair. All that is open to them is to accept the pointlessness of things and do their best to build up a world with as little evil in it as possible.

Marxists are more optimistic though, of course, they too see the wretchedness that exists, particularly in the world of labour. "The accumulation of riches at the one pole of society means an accumulation of misery, suffering and moral degradation at the other." Having diagnosed the trouble Karl Marx proceeds to provide the remedy, a false one supported by false dialectics, sociology, economics and politics. Marx explains the proletarian to himself and makes him aware of his own strength.

In fact the marxist remedy merely aggravates the evil. It denies man his value as an immortal soul, and it imprisons him in a collectivism deemed to be absolute. To understand the whole wretchedness and hopelessness of the man without God you must live for a while in a marxist atmosphere, even though marxism can certainly occasionally be a substitute for religion. From Christianity it has borrowed a certain faith in man, a certain hope in "the great tomorrow", a certain human charity and human solidarity. But, when it presents itself integrally in a collectivist society authentically applying its own doctrines it violates the liberty and integrity of the person. Women and children are its first victims, probably because they are more sensitive to personal values.

On the surface things seem perfect in such societies. The Jewish kibbutzim are an example, though they are tempered with a certain liberalism. In such societies each gives according to his possibilities and receives according to his needs. There is no exploitation of man by man at all. But the exploitation of man by the collective is worse still.

The Jewish kibbutz is a milder form of this kind of society, since its members are at least allowed to leave it if they wish. There are no other obligations but willingness and economic necessity. On the other hand, once the communist system is firmly established it is practically impossible to get out of it in any way. Where the Jewish kibbutz is concerned there is still a certain spirit of wisdom and a certain feeling for the true nature of man, which prevents an all too rigorous application of the doctrine. Incidentally, some of the kibbutzim practise the Jewish faith and this prevents them from falling into the excesses of atheistic collectivism. At the same time there is a tendency in many kibbutzim to develop towards a more human form of life, and some of them have already become co-operative villages.

Only internal developments of this nature seem likely ever to liberate the millions of people who live in collectivist countries. To dream of some sort of crusade to do away with communism is illusory, dangerous and rather unchristian. However, there is no human society which cannot be saved by the power of the Gospel.

Yet such is the situation of humanity today that a third of the sons of God live without God and without hope— not by any fault or choice of their own, but because of sociological compulsion.

Surely these people represent the lost groat that the Church must search for diligently, if necessary turning her house upside down until she has found it—a groat stamped with the effigy of her bridegroom, the carpenter Jesus of Nazareth.

The Church is in a much better position than Karl Marx to show humanity its origin and its ultimate end, its strength and its dignity, its earthly salvation and its eternal hope.

Salim, a young Christian Arab works in a marxist, atheist kibbutz: "They say there is no God. They keep on saying it, and if you ask them questions about the origin or the end of the world all they can do is to say it again. They are like those who bow down and worship a stone idol firmly believing it to be God. But their particular idol is their people, their kibbutz, their technique. Isn't it possible that they're going towards God that way just the same?"

Salim has never studied theology, but he senses that by means of this stone idol a man can open his heart to him who created the stone in the first place. Beyond man, beyond the human community, and beyond the technology of man there is the Son of Man. Will man deify himself or open his heart to the love of him who became man and dwelt amongst us? Will man make an idol of his work, or will he turn to him who works without ceasing and has revealed himself to us in the guise of a carpenter?

Will humanity deify itself as a complete and perfect thing, or will it recognize its head, Christ? To help man to find the true path the Church must proclaim the good tidings at all times to all men: Jesus is the lord of the cosmos and the saviour of man, recapitulating in himself all history and all human labour, redeeming man by his death and resurrection. The evolution of the cosmos glorifies the Creator. Should not the evolution of mankind free mankind and glorify him too? It cannot do so unless men share their goods according to the needs of each so that the whole of humanity can live, since "the Glory of God is the living man". By proclaiming the Gospel in our day the Church will save humanity from that worst of misery, atheism. As Carolina Maria de Jesus says on page 39 of her diary: "For me the world instead of evolving is turning primitive. Those who don't know hunger will say: 'Whoever wrote this is crazy.' But who has gone hungry can say: 'Well, Dona Carolina. The basic necessities must be within reach of everyone.'"

"We know that the whole creation has been groaning in

travail together until now" (Rom. 8:22). Man is waiting to be revealed to himself. May the bond be revealed to him which united the starveling, the sick, the dispossessed, the workman, even the atheist himself, with that Christ who "himself took our infirmities, and bore our diseases" (Matt. 8:17), which brought him to that exclamation on the Cross: "My God, why hast thou forsaken me?" It is the cry of so many who, in the face of so much misery feel that they cannot believe.

The Dying and the Dead

That cry of the dying Jesus: "My God, my God, why hast thou forsaken me?" sums up the supreme anguish of man faced with extreme poverty, lacking everything, his clothing, his very body itself, and his soul. And "he gave up the ghost". What else remained to him? Is it the fullness of love which receives him as the arms of a mother normally receive her new-born child? Man is naked at death as he is at birth. For one, he is wrapped in swaddling clothes, for the other he is wrapped in a winding sheet. Oriental liturgy sings of the swaddling clothes and the winding sheet together. To meditate on death or on birth, on the cradle or on the grave, is all one. Time itself, that mysterious reality that measures our life, escapes us at the hour of our death. It is then that the gates of eternity open. As soon as he is conceived the child enters into time in his mother's womb, and nine months later enters into human space for a few, short years. He "is" and he will "have" for a while. Time passes and he is no more, and he has nothing, not even this same time. One no longer says of him: he is ten, or fifty, or whatever his age; one says: he has been dead ten years, fifty years. He has passed away, entered into another world, a world of being, but no longer of having. Once again he is a being in eternity, just a being—without a bank account, without bread, without clothing, without a house, and without a body. "Fool, this night your soul is required of you: and the things you have prepared whose shall they be?" (Luke 12:20).

Man's body returns to dust. "You are dust" (Gen. 3:19). Until the resurrection of the body the soul will remain without its physical clothing. Man entire must be transfigured in immortality. This is the wages of sin. This essential poverty gives him communion at death with him who is the resurrection and the life. He wished to die and be laid in the tomb that his innumerable brothers might be brought from death to life. He descended into hell to preach the Gospel to the dead. He also "went and preached to the spirits in prison who formerly did not obey . . . (I Peter 3: 19-20). Jesus remained poor to the end of his life in order to announce the glad tidings to the dead and introduce them to life.

The gates of the kingdom are guarded by the poor and the children "for theirs is the kingdom of heaven" (Matt. 5:3). Only those will enter paradise who showed love to their brothers here below by sharing their possessions with those who were hungry . . . that is to say, with the poor man, the Son of Man, the Judge. "I was hungry and you gave me to eat. Enter. . . ."

If during this life here below a mortal has not succeeded in sharing and thus becoming poor, gentle, humble, pure, and athirst for justice, then the Merciful will allow him to go to purgatory. By purifying suffering the soul will then gain that heaven of the poor it was unable to recognize whilst here below. The heart of the rich man must be very hard indeed before the Merciful will have to say: "Depart from me, you cursed, into the eternal fire, prepared for the devil and his angels" (Matt. 25:41).

Simon Peter, who has received the keys of the kingdom of heaven, will allow only those to enter to whom Jesus can say in truth: "Blessed are the poor. . . ." And his successor on this earth, the gentle Pope John, declared again and again: "The miseries of our social life cry aloud to heaven for vengeance."

On the day that men appear naked before their Judge, many will seek to clothe themselves with their ephemeral social, political and ecclesiastical dignities, even with their alleged sense of justice or their pharisaical saintliness: "When once the householder has risen up and shut the door, you will begin to stand outside and to knock at the door, saying, 'Lord, open unto us. . . . We ate and drank in your presence, and you taught in our streets. . . . Lord, Lord, did we not prophesy in your name, and cast out demons in your name, and do many mighty works in your name?' But he will reply: 'I tell you, I do not know where you come from; depart from me, all you workers of iniquity. For I was hungry and you gave me no food. I was thirsty and you gave me no drink . . . .' 'Lord when did we see you hungry?' And he will reply: 'Truly I say to you, as you did it not to one of the least of these, you did it not to me'" (Luke 13:25-7; Matt. 7:22-3). Yet many others who believed that they could not believe and who despaired of hoping will nevertheless marvel before the Lord who is "the hope of the hopeless" (Liturgy of St Basil). They will be judged only by love. "Then the King will say to those at his right hand: 'Come, O blessed of my Father, inherit the kingdom prepared for you from the foundation of the world. For I was hungry and you gave me food. . . .' Then the righteous will answer him, 'Lord, when did we see you hungry? . . .' And the King will answer them, saying: 'Truly, I say to you, as you did it to one of the least of these, you did it to me'" (Matt. 25:34-45).

It is urgent to proclaim the Gospel to the men of our day whilst there is still time.

Of course, the Church has already spoken. It has already

done so much for the poor, the hungry, the homeless, the sick, the ignorant, children, women, the despised and rejected, the workers.... Its charity is beyond count. But what is most desirable: to do *for* or to live *with*; to speak *for* someone or to speak *with* him. Only too often good works have been performed *for* the poor. But have we experienced, suffered and worked sufficiently *with* them. Jesus became a carpenter and carried the cross. He lived with men and worked with them. He spoke the simple language of the Gospel. But when the men of the Church speak it is, alas, only too often in a language which is but little understood by the men of our day. Churchmen have not yet succeeded in spreading the whole light of Christ, the carpenter identified with the poor, over this world of labour and socialization. And what is more, their words are contradicted by the way so many of them are outwardly apparelled and by the general position they occupy in the world. Not long ago a coloured African bishop said: "I am very much embarrassed by the golden cross on my breast when I go pleading in Europe for my poor diocese. Peter and John were able to say in truth: 'Gold and silver have I none.'" Monsignor Fulton Sheen underlined another and graver aspect of the situation: "We Westerners have taken Christ, but without his cross. We have left the cross still burdening the peoples of the East. If we wish to give them Christ then we must take their cross from them and bear it ourselves."

Despite deceptive appearances, humanity today is much as it was when Jesus walked through the cities and villages: "... they were harassed and helpless, like sheep without a shepherd." And he said to his disciples: "The harvest is plentiful, but the labourers are few; pray therefore the Lord of the harvest, to send out labourers into his harvest" (Matt. 9:36-8).

II
JESUS, THE CHURCH
AND THE POOR

Jesus lived in Nazareth as a carpenter. A group of Christian workers in Nazareth, assisted by a priest, sent this appeal to their archbishop and their bishops, in order to convey to the fathers of the council the hope of the working-class world, the world of the under-privileged, the world of the poor.

They asked that under the guidance of the Holy Spirit they should consider the relation of love which unites the Church with the poor, identified with Jesus, so that when men look at the Church today they shall recognize Jesus of Nazareth, the carpenter.

Chapter Two

Jesus, the Church and the Poor

AT a moment when the bishops, the successors of the apostles, are united in council around the Vicar of Christ, these pages aim to help to make known the voice of the poor, their sufferings and their hopes.

We thought of coming to Rome to place the questions which occupy our minds before our Fathers in the faith, but, being workers, we could not leave our work. We also thought of inviting our dear Pope John XXIII to come in pilgrimage to Nazareth, but we lacked sufficient audacity, though he went to Loretto and Assisi, where he spoke of Jesus the workman.[1] And on 11 September he declared: "The Church presents herself as she is and as she desires to be: the Church of all, but particularly the Church of the poor."

Encouraged by these words we should like to invite the Fathers of the Council to look from Rome towards Nazareth, towards Jesus of Nazareth still living in the persons of the poor and of the workers.

The poor really means all men, all humanity, in the sense that all are lost by sin and called to salvation in Jesus Christ. And in an even more exact fashion the poor are all those men who realize their own human and spiritual misery, and acknowledge themselves sinners and necessitous before God, their creator and saviour, even if they are culturally

[1] And Pope Paul has since made that pilgrimage.

55

and materially rich. But the poor are, above all, those who have at the utmost just the bare necessities, or perhaps not even that—the ordinary people, the small men, the labourers, the exploited, the oppressed and, in the extreme, the starving.

These are the ones who wish to make their feelings felt here—those immense human masses who are present even in Christian countries, and who represent two-thirds of humankind.

These lines have been written in order to help find an answer to the grave question which is now facing humanity: "What is the relationship between Christianity and those peoples who have not yet heard the Gospel and are therefore ill-equipped in life? What is the relationship between the Church and the working people and the poor? What is the relationship between the poor and Jesus of Nazareth?"

These pages are addressed in all filial affection and respect, and in faith in Jesus, Pastor and Apostle, living in his hierarchical Church, to our archbishop and to our Patriarch, and through them to all the bishops and theologians brought together by our Holy Father the Pope for the hope of the whole Church. These pages are also addressed to all those contemplative religious who by their prayers turn the eyes of the Church towards her bridegroom.

Living and working in Nazareth we are confronted directly with the mystery of Jesus the carpenter, and by virtue of the practical situation which exists in Nazareth we are living amongst a mass of poor, working people, amongst Christians belonging to all the Christian Churches, surrounded and alone in a great mass of Moslems and Jews.

Although it is now true that in certain Western countries the working man is no longer poor, everywhere else he is still in a condition very close to poverty and even destitution. Writing in *Mater et Magistra*, Pope John XXIII declared: "We are filled with an overwhelming sadness when we contemplate the sorry spectacle of millions of workers in many lands and entire continents condemned through the inadequacy of their wages to live with their families in utterly sub-human conditions."[1]

Over and above this, the world of labour, even where it is no longer materially poor, remains far from the Church— sometimes even farther away than it was in the days when it was physically poor, since it is still held fast in spiritual poverty; without God and without the Gospel it is poor in all essential things.

In our day poor peoples are turning more and more to labour and to working-class organization as a means to save them from their misery. Very often they feel that their only hope lies in communism, which has succeeded in presenting itself as the conscience of the working man and of the poor.

In Nazareth we live at the divide between the world of destitution and the world of those working men who now live like human beings. We live at the frontier of the East and the West, between the past of feudalism, economic liberalism and colonialism and the future of working-class organization and socialization.

For these reasons we are speaking here of those peoples who have not been won for the Gospel, and at the same time of those peoples who are not yet developed, people of the working class, poor people. The close relationship between the world of the poor and the world of labour is recognizable even on the Gospel plane. It was here in Nazareth that Jesus entered into the world of labour as a carpenter, and into the world of the poor because of his humble social standing; he was "the common man"—as they observed with contempt, a simple Nazarene.

"The poor have not been won for the Gospel." This sad

[1] English translation, C.T.S., London, 1962 para. 68.

confession is still true today. If you look at the map of the
world you will see that generally speaking Catholic, or
Christian, countries coincide with those countries in which
ordinary people can eat their fill, whereas those countries
in which they may not are still awaiting their conversion,
or are hardly converted as yet. Latin America might seem
to be an exception to this, but to what extent can Latin
America really be regarded as won for the Gospel when
there are so few priests there? Geographically therefore we
can see a dividing line drawn between the Church, which
is well established in the more prosperous countries, and
the poor peoples of this world, who see the Church only
from the outside. On returning from New Delhi after the
World Council of Churches conference, Fr Villain
expressed his sorrow at having to admit that in those countries of famine the churches appeared as rich tourists
representing only a very small minority. The division between the churches is certainly a scandal to unbelievers
and a source of dismay for believers, who are aware of the
prayer of Christ: "That they may all be one so that the
world may believe that thou hast sent me." But the separation between the churches on the one hand and the poor
peoples of the world on the other is a much graver scandal
and a source of still keener sorrow.

The same comparison can also be made within the ancient
countries of Christianity, where only too often the Church
is firmly established in the cities, amongst the prosperous of
this world, whereas, with minor exceptions, the poor and
the working people see her only from the outside and with
little understanding. When our priests were withdrawn
from the factories in France a working woman of Lille
said: "For once the Church was with us, and now she's
going away again." Only the hierarchy can pass judgement
on the mission of its priests, and it alone can develop and
sustain it, but all the same the working people feel them-

selves abandoned without priests in their own world.

One can see the same phenomenon in countries which are still regarded as missionary, or in which Christianity is still young: the Church often seems to be associated and attached to certain economic or political power groupings, which means that the common people and the poor may perhaps be attracted to it by the hope of material advantage instead of by the Gospel. A coloured Catholic in Kenya confessed that he was scandalized to see the missionaries installed in good houses, living in reasonable comfort and at the same time announcing "Blessed are the poor" to masses of the wretched and miserable. A missionary returned from China and Viet Nam said the same thing, despite the heroism and the saintliness of so many missionaries. This is not a question of personalities but of the objective situation.

The words of Pius XI are full of profound significance: "The scandal of the twentieth century is that the Church has lost the working class." In fact, however, the Church has not lost the working class, because this new class was never inside the Church, never having been won from within. And beyond the working class are all those poor peoples, peoples who are determined to work hard to emerge from their poverty, and all those poor nations which have not yet received the light of the Gospel from the Church.

The hierarchy is established pretty well everywhere geographically but not sociologically, in which respect it seems restricted and attached to that part of the world in which men eat their fill and are clothed and housed without moiling and toiling. This world is foreign to and different from that in which two-thirds of humanity live, in which they have not bread enough either for their bodies or their souls, in which they must work hard and hope for very little return. A working-class trade-union delegate from the former Belgian Congo who was passing through Nazareth asked: "Why have the missionaries made us lose the faith they brought us in the first place? Why are their standards of living in our country so far above ours, and so far above those of the Gospel? And yet it was here that the Word was made flesh."

Jesus gave as a sign of his messianism that "the poor have good news preached to them" (Luke 7:22). Is this same sign sufficiently obvious in our day? If it were merely a question of some delay in the winning of the newly arisen peoples, of the newly founded nations, it would not be so bad; but what in fact, we are talking about is the poor and the rupture between them and the Church's outward appearance. Poor people do not feel themselves at home in the Church. "Why do the priests want to make themselves greater than God?" an Arab Christian workman of Nazareth asked sorrowfully—precisely because of this scandal he had strayed for a time into the camp of militant communism. "Have the bishops themselves the faith?" demanded a Jew acquainted with churchmen; and he continued: "You don't have to have the faith to live the way they do. They lack nothing. . . ."

Saint Bernard and Catherine of Siena have both spoken in the same strain; and in a letter dated 7 July 1962 and sent out on the eve of the Council to all religious all over the world, Pope John pointed out that poverty could not readily be reconciled with "ostentation in buildings and accommodation, such as has already attracted unfavourable comment in some cases". The Christian workmen of Nazareth sadly confirm this contradiction.

Sami Khoury, an Orthodox Christian, a fitter, says: "The churches are interested only in the rich and the bourgeois. If a worker or a poor man fails to go to church no one bothers, but if a rich man or a bourgeois fails to go, then people get upset. Poor people aren't accepted in the

Church, and they feel that they are looked down on with contempt."

Abou Bchara, Latin rite, an old building workman, says: "Much more important than building houses for the poor, much more important than pushing on with the work in the co-operatives, is to save the tree of our faith which has been planted in this ground. This tree is ailing today, and we have to watch over the faith of our children, whom too many things in our churches scandalize."

Bchara, chairman of a small building co-operative, Latin rite: "When I was still at school I often calculated how many houses you could build for the poor just with one wall of the religious building near us."

Bassem, building worker, Greek Catholic: "Of course the religious serve God and the people with their prayers, their schools and their hospitals. But why those large landed holdings which take up room working people would like for their homes. The ground around these religious houses is largely left untilled."

It is easy for communist propaganda to seize on this sort of thing, but before we begin to accuse these workers of communism it would be a good idea to ask whether this "unfavourable comment" has not been caused by the "ostentation" Pope John refers to in his letter.

The fact that there is a chasm between the hierarchical Church and poor people is a scandal every bit as great as the disunity of the churches, because it too is a schism, a gash in the body of Christ. Jesus is, in fact, indissolubly one both with his Church and with the poor.

The identification of Jesus with his Church has been expressed in particular since the development of the theological idea of the Mystical Body and of the Church. Thus in the encyclical *Mystici Corporis*, Pius XII explained just how Jesus lives in his Church: "Christ lives so fully in his Church that it is like another presence. . . . However, this noble description should not be understood to mean that the ineffable bond by which the Son of God took an actual human nature extends to the whole Church, but in the sense that Our Saviour lends his Church all those things which are right and proper so that in her mode of life, both visible and invisible, she may represent the image of Christ with the utmost possible perfection."

1. *Jesus and the Poor*

The Gospel and the epistles are clear on the identification of Jesus with the poor, and the spiritual and mystical tradition is strong and undeviating. However, the theological expression of this truth is not as yet very vigorously developed. The Abbé Pierre raised the point again recently: "I have been struck by the similarity of the words our Lord uses in the Gospel to institute the sacrament of the eucharist, and I should like our theologians to analyse this for us in all possible detail—this is *my* body—and the words he uses when speaking of the sufferers at the Last Judgement: 'I was hungry. I was cold. I. . . .' One can almost compare the words: 'He who heareth you, heareth me,' and, again: 'Inasmuch as ye did it to one of the least of these, ye did it unto me.'" Certainly, the identification of Jesus with his Church, with his eucharistic body, is not identical with his identification with the poor, but there remains a bond which it is important to clarify because it would further the conversion of the poor, and reinforce the social doctrine of the Church, and her way of life, which should represent the image of Christ, his body, his bride, and reproduce in "her mode of life, both visible and invisible, the image of Christ".[1]

The Gospel clearly shows that Jesus desired to be poor, that he identified himself with the poor.

[1] Pius XII, see above

(a) Jesus lived as a poor man

Jesus was born poor and died in poverty and destitution. One might perhaps have thought that the Word made flesh would have chosen to be born in a palace, or at least in a reasonably comfortable house. But he was born in a stable. At the end of his life he was crucified "outside the city". For thirty years before this he lived as a member of a poor family of artisans in a small village, and when he grew old enough to work he plied the trade of a carpenter. The priest of priests willed to live and work as a rural worker. All his life and all his teachings were marked by his origin and his condition. He spoke and acted like a carpenter. He was not a prophet from noble Judea, but from humble Galilee. He was dressed just as all the other people of his humble world were dressed—he dressed like a working man, and not in purple. He lived in an ordinary simple house and not in a palace. When a French working woman heard that the French worker priests were no longer to be allowed to work she said: "But Christ was a workman, wasn't he? And he didn't change; he stayed a workman to the end. . . ."

When Jesus revealed his messianity in the synagogue in Nazareth he presented himself as consecrated by the spirit of the Lord "to preach the Gospel to the poor" (Luke 4:18). People knew him as a carpenter and the son of a carpenter. In the same way, at the moment when he revealed himself as the "Christ", the Messiah, the consecrated one, the one who had been sent, he showed the connection between this consecration and mission on the one hand, and the poor to whom he had been sent and for whom he had been consecrated, on the other. Thus in his innermost being Jesus revealed himself as attached to the poor. What is this mysterious bond between the consecration and the mission of Jesus on the one hand, and the poor to whom the Gospel was to be preached on the other. The poor in question represented, of course, the whole of humanity, and Jesus had not come in the first place to resolve social problems. However, it remains true that humanity cannot be saved except through Jesus Christ, who made himself poor, and who addressed himself by preference to the poor, to peasants and working men, to ordinary folk.

(b) Jesus identified himself with the poor

Poor himself, Jesus identified himself in a mysterious fashion with the poor of all time, and he did this clearly and solemnly (Matt. 25). The Son of Man, coming in all his glory, identified himself with the hungry and the thirsty, with those who were sick and in rags, with those who were prisoners, and those who were homeless ... that is to say, he identified himself with all those who lived in extreme poverty, destitution, and urgent necessity. Without even knowing him for what he was, things could be done for him by being done for them. Thus in a mysterious fashion Christ lived in them. Unquestionably as a divine person Jesus is distinct from the poor; and both his physical and eucharistic body were entitled to the homage paid to it by Mary of Bethany with her costly ointment of spikenard "for the day of my burial" (John 12:7). His physical presence is not permanently there for the Christian to love, but the poor, the social body of Christ, are always with us to be loved and helped (Mark 14:7). Mary of Bethany's gesture and the reply Jesus made to Judas very clearly reveal the nature of Jesus' identity with the poor on the one hand, and of Jesus with the hierarchical Church on the other. It is not a question of any physical identity. And it is also not a vague moral identity. Jesus did not say: "Inasmuch as you do it to the least of these it is *as though* you did it to me." Again, he did not say: "This is *as though it were* my body," nor "for those who hear you it is *as though* they hear me". No,

Jesus said: "You do this to me", "This is my body", and "He who hears you hears me". Of course, the identification is different in each case: real eucharistic presence, mystic ecclesiastical presence, and social presence. In all three cases the presence is mysterious and real, implying that Jesus is the man for all men, but in particular and especially for the suffering and the poor. In all three cases it is Jesus who by his own desire and love sustains the mysterious attachment, the mysterious identification. And since Jesus is at the heart of these relationships, the three cannot be separated: the eucharist is in and for the Church, the poor are in the Church as of right, and the Church is there to save them. The eucharist fulfils itself in the breaking of bread. In the days of early Christianity the celebration expressly included the offering and its distribution amongst the poor. Ultimately, the heavenly Church will assemble in Christ all those who have given him to eat and to drink here below, all those who have clothed and lodged, received and loved him in the person of the necessitous and the heavy laden. "Come, O blessed of my Father, inherit the kingdom prepared for you" (Matt. 25:34).

The parable of the rich man and Lazarus (Luke 26:19) shows how when he died the poor man was carried by angels up to heaven, being identified with Christ glorious, because, without even knowing it, he had borne the burden of misery, injustice and sin in this life: Lazarus received evil things during his lifetime, "but now he is comforted" (Luke 16:25). And the last words of Jesus, risen from the dead, once more underlined his identity with the persecuted: "I am Jesus whom you are persecuting" (Acts. 9:5).

The Epistle of St James affirms the same truth in very decided terms: "The faith of our Lord Jesus Christ, the Lord of glory" demands that the eminent dignity of the poor should be recognized, even "in shabby clothing", rather

3

than that "the man with gold rings" and "in fine clothing" should be so honoured (James 2:1-3), the man who oppresses and blasphemes that worthy name (ibid., 6-7). It was the rich who condemned and put the Just one (Jesus) to death, and who go on condemning and killing whilst heaping up gold and wealth and defrauding labourers of their wages (ibid., 4). Thus James identifies Jesus with the poor man "in shabby clothing", who is rejected and despised and defrauded of his wages. The Judge stands before the door (Ibid. 5:9) and identifies himself with the exploited worker, and the Son of Man identifies himself with the hungry (Matt. 25:35 ff).

(c) *Spiritual tradition identifies Jesus with the poor*

A whole spiritual tradition stemming from the Gospel identifies Jesus with the poor and has encouraged not only the humble service of the poor but the identification of the poor by communion with Jesus. It was to Saint Martin the catechumen that Jesus appeared dressed in the one half of the mantle that Saint Martin had given to the beggar. Saint Julian the Hospitaller embraced the leper, who was revealed as Christ the glorious and carried him up to heaven in his arms. Saint John the Almoner, appointed Patriarch of Alexandria, immediately declared that he must visit his masters and his helpers, that is to say, the poor, because they are Jesus himself and they alone can give the kingdom of heaven. This same John the Almoner tells an illuminating story of the tax collector, Peter, who tossed a piece of bread to a beggar in order to get rid of him, and subsequently in a dream saw himself saved from hell by that one piece of bread. He then deemed it prudent to give his shirt to a poor man without one, whereupon Jesus appeared to him wearing the shirt, as he had appeared to Saint Martin of Tours wearing the half cloak. At that his eyes were opened and he decided that "Since Jesus lived in the person of the poor he would become one of them before he died". So he allowed himself to be sold into slavery and had the purchase price distributed amongst the poor. Jesus then recognized him as his brother, saying: "Peter, my brother, I have received the money for which you were sold." John the Almoner also tells us how Saint Serapion sold his Bible and then sold himself in order to live the Bible and commune with Jesus. The same communion can be seen in the kiss given to the leper by Saint Francis of Assisi. Vincent de Paul taught his daughters to recognize their master Jesus in the poor: "A poor peasant or a poor woman ... are coarse and earthy. Yet turn to the other side of the medallion and you will see by the light of faith that the Son of God, who desired to be poor, is represented to us by these poor people" (*Fragment* 165). Bossuet sees in the poor man "the living and speaking likeness bearing the natural expression of the dying Jesus.... Jesus suffering in the poor, patient in the poor". For Lacordaire "the poor man is a living crucifix". The same vision accompanied Père de Foucauld from the day he discovered Jesus before the corpse of a poor worker who had died of hunger. According to the Abbé Chocarne, who founded an order of Dominican Sisters, Jesus desired to have two sacrifices of himself on this earth, the one in which he gives himself as nourishment —the eucharist—and the other by which he is nourished —the poor.

Beyond community of destiny with the world of labour, which waits to be saved, surely the worker-priests were seeking communion with Jesus living in his working members cruelly separated from the Church. It was certainly what Monsignor Tulia Botera Salazar, Archbishop of Medelline in Columbia, was seeking when, having distributed all his possessions amongst the poor, he turned his palace into a workers' university, and went out to a distant poor suburb to live in poverty and thus feel himself nearer to Jesus.[1] Peter Claver vowed that he would become a slave of the Negroes for the rest of his life. When the Abbé Pierre called on the theologians to clarify the identity of Jesus with the poor it was because this self-same identity of love had transformed his own life and removed the layers of egoism which had enveloped him.

Why did Jesus identify himself with the poor? Perhaps because together with him they carry the burden of this world's sin, because they are more closely associated with the Redemption, both as saved and saviours?

Have they not, indeed, a privileged place in the Mystical Body, a place that theology must now assign them?

Possessing no material wealth and having no bank account, the poor man, like the child, reminds the world of the primacy of being over having. And perhaps that is another reason why Jesus desired to identify himself with the child and with the poor man: "What doth it profit a man if he gain the whole world and suffer the loss of his own soul?"

On account of this primacy of being over having, and on account of the Redemption, Jesus has established that mysterious relationship between them and him.

Until it is clearly laid down by the Church, this truth will be grotesquely distorted in that mystique and dialectic which turn the proletarian and the child into idols, whereas Jesus Christ alone can confer on them their authentic worth as human beings and their Redemption in him.

2. *The Poor and the Church*

Since Jesus has identified himself on the one hand with his Church and on the other hand with the poor it would be logical to conclude that there is an identity between the

[1] *Informations Catholiques Internationales,* 1 July 1962, p. 10

Church and the poor. But these two identifications—
Jesus = the Church, and Jesus = the poor—are not inter-
changeable, each being "a partial identity" only, like the
identification of man and woman in marriage, which does
not absorb the person of each, but fulfils them both. It is
therefore important to consider in what form Jesus desired
this identity of the Church and the poor.

(a) *Poor people; the servant of Yahweh, in the Old Testament*

God willed Israel, prefiguration of the Church, to be the
people of the poor. Israel was a small nation amongst vast
empires, without much culture, without great economic or
military strength. Just because of this Israel was the sacrament of God amongst the peoples in the expectation of the
Perfect Sacrament, the Consecrated One, the Messiah,
Jesus of Nazareth. When Israel was in danger of
contamination by contact with the great, God sent Israel
into the desert and there, in poverty, he "spoke his heart"
to the bride, his first Church, the Church of the desert.
God permitted Israel to be carried off and reduced to a
condition of slavery so that it might remain King, and there
in deprivation Israel sang those songs in which it describes
itself as the servant of Yahweh, a suffering servant, identified with the Messiah and consecrated by the spirit to
preach the Gospel to the poor (Is. 61). The danger of riches
for Israel is summed up in the story of the golden calf.
"Israel has become fat and sated and has abandoned its
God." It was Karl Marx who wrote: "Money is the jealous
God of Israel"; the false god that provokes divine vengeance; that is to say, the ruin of a people without God. Hence
the invective of the prophet against riches and the rich
(Is. 3:14; Amos. 2:6-7), invective whose only purpose is a
moral one, since it seeks to save the mystery of the election

of Yahweh's poor people, of his servant. The election of
Israel as Yahweh's servant is related to the mystery of
the poor of Yahweh, the servant of Yahweh, the one and the
other prefiguring and preparing the way for the servant
Jesus. Israel had to become the poor people of Yahweh in
order to conform with the Messiah as the Church must
conform with Jesus.

(b) *In the Gospel the kingdom belongs to the poor*

Jesus describes the Church in terms of the kingdom, and
of the reign of God, as a great parable of the mystery of his
love gathering redeemed humanity to himself. Now this
kingdom belongs to the poor. But it is the heart that counts,
and only those possess the kingdom who have the spirit of
the poor (Matt. 5:3). And Luke refers to the poor, the
ordinary people, the great multitudes coming together to
hear, and to be healed by him of their infirmities (Luke
5:15), those who are hungry now, those who weep and are
rejected. To be poor normally ensures that man is ready for
salvation: poverty makes him detached, humble, receptive, sick, fit to be saved. On the other hand, the rich man
is in a dangerous state, because he has received his consolation here below (Luke 5:27). He is sated, content, looked
up to, and so he is not ready to be saved. It will be as difficult for him to enter heaven as it is for a camel to go through
the eye of a needle (Luke 18:25; Matt. 19:24; Mark 10:24).
The parable of Dives and Lazarus underlines this difference
and this reversal of the situation (Luke 16:19 ff). The parable of the rich man who laid up worldly goods condemns
this false confidence (Luke 12:16 ff). "You cannot serve God
and mammon" since mammon is unrighteous (Luke 16:11,
13). Wealth can be made righteous only in the service of the
poor (Luke 16:1-15). The poor will enjoy riches when they
are received into everlasting habitations (Luke 16:9). Jesus,

the poor man, will judge men by their attitude to the poor, the possessors of the kingdom of heaven (Matt. 25:31 ff). Those who are called upon to enter the kingdom by a shorter route, by evangelic perfection, must sell all they have and give it to the poor. At death all are poor, and purgatory is there to bring the heart into line.

(c) *Jesus founded his Church on the poor*

The apostles were not destitute, but they were poor men who worked hard for their living. "Master, we toiled all night, and took nothing" (Luke 5:5) was Peter's reply when Jesus wished to engage him and his three companions to work henceforth as fishers of men. Matthew himself was "sitting at the tax office" (Luke 5:27), and without further ado, without talking about it, Jesus said: "Follow me". He was to leave all that, abandon his way of earning a living, and follow Jesus, and so he did. Amongst Jesus' friends there were certainly some who were in easier circumstances: Lazarus and his sisters, Joseph of Arimathea, Nicodemus, and a number of women. But Jesus founded his Church only on working men and it was these he called to be his apostles.

Sometimes in the Gospel it is difficult to tell whether the disciples themselves or the poor in general are under discussion; when, for example, Jesus says: "As you did it to one of the least of these, you did it to me." In certain cases he clearly means the disciples, those who represent him, those in whom he lives since they are members of his hierarchical Church, composed of apostles and believers (Matt. 10:40-42; John 13:20; Luke 10:16).

Elsewhere Jesus identifies himself with little children, whom he takes into his arms and blesses (Mark 9:37; Luke 9:48). But in these cases Jesus presents the child as an example to the apostles in order that they should become as little children themselves, and not great men, which was their secret ambition (Mark 9 : 33 ff; Luke 9 : 46 ff).

And finally Jesus identifies himself with the poor, with those who are hungry, ragged, sick and prisoners. . . . "I was hungry. . . . As you did it to one of the least of these. . . ." (Matt. 25:34-40). Those who gave him food did not do so in the persons of his recognized disciples since they were astonished: "When did we give you food?" They had merely helped the poor. And yet the disciples are obviously meant here, because Jesus instructs his apostles and disciples that they themselves cannot be anything but hungry, poorly clothed and persecuted. "Take no gold, nor silver, nor copper in your belts . . . eat and drink whatever they provide. . . . They will lay their hands on you . . . delivering you . . . into prisons (Matt. 10 : 9-17; Luke 10 : 4-7; 21 : 12). In this way the disciples and the apostles are simultaneously identified with the working and suffering Jesus and with all those who work and suffer.

To suppose that with these words Jesus does nothing but affirm his identification with his disciples is to forget that the servant is not greater than his master (John 15 : 20), and may not be identified with him until he is obedient to his word. It is this that makes him one with those who labour and are poor.

(d) *Jesus gave instructions to his Church: "Take no gold or silver"*

The group of apostles around Jesus had a common purse of which Judas was in charge. Jesus was given shelter and hospitality by the well-to-do. This removes all inflexibility, intransigence and sectarianism from poverty. Jesus never speaks in an abstract and inflexible fashion about poverty.

The common purse of the brethren was available to the

poor (John 13:29). Jesus never demanded that contributions should be made to it, and it must have been kept filled by the group of apostles themselves and by the women.

Again, Jesus never demanded perfect poverty of everyone. Nowhere does he speak of it. What counted was the poor, preaching the Gospel to the poor, and service of the poor.

Jesus gave one instruction for the apostolic life: "no gold nor silver" (Luke 9:1-3; 10:4; Matt. 10:5-9; Mark 6:8-13). The apostles were entitled to take from those to whom they preached the Gospel, or to work with their hands, or live from the common purse. The Gospel itself was free. "You received without pay; give without pay." This is the sign of true love: gratuity. It is the sign of him who, being rich, made himself poor for love (II Cor. 8:9). It is the essential power of the Gospel. Peter, who said to the lame man at the gate of the temple which is called Beautiful: "Gold and silver have I none" understood this very well (Acts 3:6).

Should his disciples not be faithful to the will of their Master, should they not be identified with him, would they still be his witnesses? If the eucharistic bread became corrupt it would cease to be the Real Presence of the Lord. If Judas baptized that baptism would be valid, but what apostolic witness could Judas provide?

(e) *The evangelical signs of the Church: the sharing of property; the preaching of the Gospel to the poor; her unity*

To the people who asked him, saying: "What shall we do?" John the Baptist replied: "He who has two coats, let him share with him who has none; and he who has food, let him do likewise" (Luke 3:10). In the same way Jesus promised the kingdom of God to him who had fed and clothed him in this life (Matt. 25:31 ff). Break bread with the hungry. Such is the morality of the prophets, and it is also the sign of the Church herself: the breaking of bread.

Replying to the messengers of John the Baptist, who asked whether he was truly the one who was to come, Jesus gave us a number of signs, the last of which was the clearest: the Gospel was being preached to the poor. If this were not so Jesus would not have been the Messiah, the Church would not have been his Church, because he is sent to preach the Gospel to the poor, and the Church extends his mission. But how should the Gospel be preached to the poor if those who are already rich with the Gospel do not share the bread of life and of the soul with those who have neither the Gospel nor bread?

And finally, the supreme sign of unity cannot be present if the body of Christ is divided: its ecclesiastical and baptized body on the one hand, and its suffering and labouring body on the other. "That they may be one that the world may see that thou has sent me." Perhaps it will be through the desire to manifest the unity of the body ecclesiastical and the body social and poor that the churches will find their unity at last. The commandment to love God and men is the law of the Church herself. Obeyed to the extent of sharing this world's goods it would bring about unity, signified by the breaking of bread. Then the Gospel would be preached to the poor.

(f) *The eminent dignity of the poor in the Church*

The first church of Jerusalem so clearly understood the will of Jesus, and lived so fully in his spirit, that "all who believed were together and had all things in common; and they sold their possessions and goods and distributed them to all, as any man had need" so that "there was not a needy person among them" (Acts 2:44; 4:34). And this was so important that to cheat in this respect was a sin against the

Holy Spirit. Peter had no indulgence for Ananias and Sapphira.

In organizing the great collection amongst the churches in aid of the church of Jerusalem, Paul launched the idea of aid to the under-developed communities as an act of faith in Jesus Christ and in his Church. "For you know the grace of our Lord Jesus Christ, that though he was rich, yet for your sake he became poor, so that by his poverty you might become rich. . . . But as a matter of equality, your abundance at the present time should supply their want, that there may be equality" (II Cor. 8 : 9-14).

On this plane there would no longer be necessitous poor, since all would be equal in a poor Church in which, how-ever, the necessity of all would be supplied. Humanity would then be a fraternal city in which each man was poor, but in which the necessities of each were supplied, as in a monastery.

Alas! only too often "one is hungry and another is drunk", despising the Church of God and blind to the Body of the Saviour (I Cor. 11 : 21, 29). The eucharist should embrace the sharing of the bread of life and the bread of the soul in the same act of faith.

"Has not God chosen those who are poor in the world to be rich in faith, and heirs of the kingdom which he has promised to those who love him? But you have dishonoured the poor man. Is it not the rich who oppress you, is it not they who drag you into court? Is it not they who blaspheme that honourable name by which you are called? . . . . Come now, you rich, weep and howl for the miseries that are coming upon you. Your riches have rotted. . . . Your gold and silver have rusted, and their rust will be evidence against you. . . . Behold the wages of the labourers who mowed your fields, which you kept back by fraud, cry out" (James 2 : 5; 5:1 ff).

The Fathers of the Church have never ceased to preach

in this spirit, denouncing the egoism of the rich, and demanding that the goods of this world shall be shared in a community of possessions. Why? Not on account of any philosophical, economic or social theory, but through that act of faith. The poor, the privileged members of Jesus, have an eminent place in the Church, which cannot afford not to conform with her master and bridegroom, Jesus of Nazareth.

The history of Charlemagne tells us of Aygolant, a Moslem chief who desired to become a Christian and was received by the Emperor. He saw the knights, the bishops and the monks sitting around the Emperor at his table, and they were presented to him as the dignitaries of the Church. He also saw that there were poor people sitting on the floor and feeding on the scraps from the table. "Who are they?" he demanded. A monk replied: "They are Jesus, who said: 'I was hungry and ye gave me to eat.'" whereupon the Moslem chief retired, greatly scandalized.

In fact the place of the poor in the Church is very different; it is that which Bossuet assigned to them in his sermon on the eminent dignity of the poor in the Church: "God has appointed those poor you despise to be his treasurers and his revenue collectors. He desires that you should give into their hands all that money which should enter into his coffers. . . . The first Church was founded only for the poor, and they are the true citizens of that happy city that the Bible has called the City of God. . . . Grace belongs by right to the poor, and the rich will receive it only from their hands. . . . The Church of Jesus Christ is truly the city of the poor. The rich, in their quality as rich, are there only on sufferance, and it is the poor and the indigent, who bear the stigmata of the Son of God, who are properly entitled to be received there."

The gesture of Monsignor Sales, Bishop of Natal in Brazil, by which he stopped the building of his new cathedral to build a workmen's city instead, is part and parcel of the same age of faith. "It is more important to build the cathedral of souls."

The social doctrine of the Church, embodied in the great encyclicals from *Rerum Novarum* to *Mater et Magistra* re-affirm and develop these same truths in the name of the same act of faith. The Church cannot fail "to make the sufferings, the plaints and the aspirations of the poor and the oppressed her own" (*Mater et Magistra*) because she says with her master and her bridegroom: "As you have done it to the least of these, you have done it to me." It necessarily recalls the words of St John and applies them to the needs of the present day and gives them a world-wide application: "But if anyone has the world's goods, and sees his brother in need, yet closes his heart against him, how does God's love abide in him?" (I John 3:17, quoted in *Mater et Magistra* in connection with the duty of the developed countries towards the under-developed countries).

The Church and the poor really form only one body, the body of Christ. This is certainly what Jesus wanted, and it is equally certain that it has always been what the Church has experienced and affirmed in her tradition. The identification of Jesus and the poor is reflected in his Church, which is identical with her bridegroom and identical with her most dearly-loved members.

As the priests of the *Mission de France*, approved by their Superiors, but torn between their obedience to their bishop and their loyalty to the world of the poor, said to their parishioners: "There must be no trickery, because it is the same Jesus Christ in his Church and in the poor who has promised that he would be with us all days even unto the end of the world."[1]

---

[1] *Informations Catholiques Internationales*, August 1962, p. 9.

3. *The Hope of the Poor*

How does it come about that there should seem, outwardly, to be an estrangement, a gap between the Church and the poor? And how grave such a rupture would be if it were to become worse!

Every risk of a breach in the body of Christ which is his Church is a very grave matter indeed, because the Church is one, and her unity is a sign of the messianism and the mission of Jesus: "That they may be one, that the world may know that Thou hast sent me."

In fact, the missionary efforts of the Church have brought the churches to a more profound realization of the scandal their divisions represent, and have given rise to the ecumenical movement. "How much can Jesus really mean to you?" ask the Jews of Nazareth of both the Orthodox and the Catholics. "Why, you have different dates to celebrate his birth, and different dates to celebrate his resurrection! And what are all your churches worth since you haven't one in which you can all worship together!"

The scandal is real, because each schism and each heresy changes the face of the Church. Of course, the Church remains one and holy in her identity with Jesus, but the world no longer sees this intimate unity. The world sees only the divisions and is rightly scandalized in consequence, because it is the sins of men which have, in various ways, torn Christendom apart.

The same thing applies to the world of the poor and of the workers. When they look at the Church, or the churches, they are scandalized by what they see—not only by the disunity but even more by the obvious breach between the world of the poor, which they represent, on the one hand, and the Church and the churches, on the other. The Church even appears to them to be on the other side of the barricade and actually allied with the world of finance and politics.

78

Of course, they frequently have reason to see that some priests are nevertheless close to them—their parish priests and curates. These are simple men, and poor men like themselves, but even these priests seem attached to that other and different world which, only too often, maintains churchmen. In addition, these priests are not the Church. The Church is represented by the bishops and by the Vatican for Catholics, by the bishops and the patriarchs for the Orthodox, and by their pastors for the Protestants. Observing that the heads of the Church do not live as Jesus of Nazareth lived, the poor and the working people turn away in disappointment and with the feeling that they have been betrayed.

"The Church of Jesus Christ continues to compromise herself with the upholders of a civilization of power and riches, whilst the labouring masses are building up a different civilization through the action of the working-class movement. Labour will be re-valued in that civilization, and working men will take the place rightly due to them in the country and in the world. Will the Church of Christ be present there to fulfil her mission of justice, unity and love, and ensure that this stream shall remain as unsullied as possible? Or will she swim against the stream with the upholders of the established order, with those who are satisfied with things as they are?" Such are the questions being asked by Christian workers in Europe,[1] and they are also being asked by Christian working men in Israel, a country in which a new world is being built up, socially inspired by the morality of the Old Testament prophets. "Workers of Nazareth, we feel ourselves at one with him who out of his love became a simple carpenter, and we are challenged by those who see the Church from outside and find that she does not conform to Jesus of Nazareth."

After he had read *Mater et Magistra* a working man in

[1] *Informations Catholiques Internationales*, August 1962, p. 10.

Nazareth demanded: "Well, why don't they practise what they preach?" The leading Moslem of Nazareth commented: "I admire the Church and I love Jesus. I have read *Mater et Magistra* with joy. But why does the Church not put what Pope John says into practice?" One parish priest was unwilling to circulate that encyclical for fear of putting his bishop in an unfavourable light. In particular it is the Church's property which gives occasion for scandal, and the way of life of her bishops, and the privileged association of high prelates with rich people. . . . A Jewish trade-union delegate who had travelled in Europe declared on his return: "Everywhere I saw that religion is allied with the rich. Working men find that it has no relation to their life." On his death-bed an old miner prayed with deep and simple faith, and one of the Little Sisters of the Poor who was acting as a nurse, proposed that she should send for a priest to which he replied: "Bring a priest to visit me now that I am sick and in pain? No, Sister, it's my friends and comrades I want to have visit me. The men who showed an interest in me during my life. The priest isn't a friend or comrade of mine. He never showed any interest in me, and now I'm not interested in him."

That wound strikes the body of Christ at a point where it is most vulnerable, because it is the very heart of Jesus which is being torn and divided, his love for his hierarchical and sacramental Church, and his love for the poor and those who are privileged by Redemption. It is a schism in the true meaning of the term, a wound in the body of Jesus, a separation of the two objects of his single, divine love.

The "schism" has become a heresy, just as in the sixteenth century the break-away of the Western countries, scandalized by the riches of Renaissance Rome and the traffic in indulgences, was bound up with the Protestant heresy. To-day the heresy is more directly connected with the mystery of poverty, which is being profaned by marxism's idolatry of the proletariat in compensation for the contempt and injustices shown by a society that called itself Christian towards the poor worker of the nineteenth century. Marxism has exalted the proletariat and cut the bond between the poor and the Church, between the poor and Christ. What is at stake is the identity of Jesus with the poor, and of the Church with the poor and with Jesus.

Now this identity is not only insufficiently visible, but we must ask ourselves whether it is being properly treated as an essential aspect of the mystery of Christ, in modern spirituality or in modern theology. It is not easy to find spiritual works which present the mystery of Jesus the Carpenter, Jesus the poor man, as a profound subject for contemplation. And it is even more difficult to obtain a definite theological answer to the question : what exactly is the identity of Jesus with the poor, and the identity of the Church with the poor? In putting the question at all you run the risk of being regarded as partisan and exaggerated, as wishing to reject the riches of the Church. And yet John Chrysostom and Saint Basil were very definite on the point. . . .

In the meantime the poor and the working people, who represent two-thirds of humanity, are still awaiting both the Gospel and the breaking of bread—both the bread of the body and the bread of the soul. They are still awaiting a gesture of friendliness from a world that calls itself Christian, and a hope of emerging from their misery; and in the absence of this gesture and this hope they are turning in despair to another hope, a very terrestrial one, that of marxism.

Incidentally, they are not asking for charity or alms. They want to work for their living. Why don't those Christians who are already well-provided stretch out a fraternal hand to their brothers in those countries which are not yet provided for and not yet won for the Gospel, as was the case with the working city of Nazareth? Big international organizations are occupying themselves with this sort of thing, of course, but nothing can replace the personal brotherly spirit witnessed by that collection St Paul organized for the Church of Jerusalem. The work of the *Secours Catholique*, and of *Misereor* and *Caritas* represents a step in the right direction, like that of the Amos Fraternity, originally founded to come to the aid of the poor in Nazareth.

In their labour, working people hope for the presence of Christ and his Church in the person of her priests; they hope that at least some priests will work and suffer with them as Jesus the Carpenter did. Working people hope to find "brothers" and "sisters" in working priests, a kind of apostolic deacon—men who will live with them, suffer with them, preach the Gospel to them, and live the Gospel in their own lives right up to and including its practical social consequences. Even a marxist kibbutz Jew calls for this presence of the Church. This evangelical leaven will give rise to whatever is requisite in any particular circumstances, such as was the case in the workers' city of Nazareth.[1]

Pius XI concluded his Encyclical on communism, *Divini Redemptoris*, by exhorting priests: "Go especially among the workers; go to all the poor...." Owing to a lack of suitable training and sufficient encouragement the worker-priest experiment in France has been discontinued, but whilst it lasted it gave rise to a great wave of hope amongst working men and poor people. "You are my brother, Father," as a working man in Nazareth said to a worker-priest. "You are doing what Jesus did, and that's right," said another. Small groups of priests and laymen dedicated to Jesus for preaching the Gospel to the poor would fulfil the expectations of working men and poor

[1] See below, Part III.

people, and make it possible to preach the Gospel to the world of labour.

But all such efforts would be in vain unless the whole Church—given a lead from above—were to set an example. This is what the Archbishop of Medelline said very clearly, suiting the action to the word: "Those who now doubt will have to bow to the evidence, and this evidence must come from above, from the source itself, from the Holy Spirit whose mission it is to govern the Church of Christ, from the chief of the archdiocese himself. It is for this reason that your own archbishop has decided to give up his comfortable residence and turn it into a school for leaders of the working men and the peasants ... and to go himself and live in a modest house in the heart of the working-class quarters."

The hope of poor people is primarily and above all to meet Jesus of Nazareth, the Carpenter, living in his Church, to be able to recognize him in recognizing his Church. Working men and poor people do not want a Church that calls itself the bride of Christ in theory whilst in practice she plays the great lady, surrounded by courtiers, goes about dressed in purple and fine linen, and living like the rich man in the parable of Dives and Lazarus. They want a Church which is really and truly identical with Jesus of Nazareth. Should a bride dress and live in any other way but that which is pleasing to her bridegroom?

This is the form of adaptation which is real and urgent for the Church: she must adapt herself, not to an epoch, but to the will of Jesus. The Church is not called upon to adapt herself to the world of labour, but to strip off her rich clothing, since this is what prevents her from appearing in truth as the bride of Christ the Carpenter. The identification of Jesus and his Church, of Jesus and the poor, would then be made manifest to all, and the poor would be won for the Gospel.

To observe the reaction amongst working men and poor people to the least gesture made in this direction is enough to tell us in advance what a united movement of the episcopate in the same direction would do. The experiment of the worker-priests in France and elsewhere; the great progress made by the Little Brothers and Sisters of Jesus; the action of Mgr Ancel in Lyons, where he went to live and work in the working-class quarter; the Worker Mission of SS. Peter and Paul at Port Bouc, continuing the dockyard work of Father Jacques Loew at Marseilles; the appeal of the Abbé Pierre; the heartening gesture of Mgr Sales in Brazil, where he preferred to build a workers' city rather than turn his living church into a great and disproportionate cathedral of stone; the similar gesture of Mgr Tulio Bodero Salazar in Columbia, leaving his episcopal palace to live near Jesus in the workers' quarters; the attitude of a good many of the clergy during the recent strikes in Spain; the simple, human and benevolent attitude of the late Pope John XXIII. All these things have been noted, taken to heart, and commented on with hope by working people even in countries which are far off, such as here in Nazareth.

The outer adaptation, the clear resemblance of the visible Church to Jesus of Nazareth, the Carpenter, and through him with the whole world of labour, and all poor and working people, can be made manifest only if the Church first contemplates her bridegroom in all the realism of his redeeming incarnation. Our religious contemplatives bear a great responsibility within the Church for her intimate communion with Jesus. If they contemplate Jesus with love as the carpenter they will cause the heart of the Church to beat in rhythm with the word of labour. If they contemplate Jesus as a Jew they will eliminate anti-semitism and prepare the reception of Israel into the Church. If they contemplate him as a man of the East they will open the eastern doors of the Church for the entry of the peoples of the East. It is important that the contemplation of all within the Church should be properly directed and closely centred on the true face of Jesus. Our epoch more than any other needs to look into the face of the carpenter.

The setting out of the identity of the Church and the poor in Jesus depends equally on exegesis and theology. Instead of eliminating the social aspect of the message in our commentaries on the Scriptures and on the Gospel, why not underline it, increase its profundity, and make it more explicit? From the Magnificat to the Epistle of St James, and including the Beatitudes, there is sufficient to accord with and justify the hopes of working men and poor people. If we let them know in detail about the experiences of the Saints, St Martin and Vincent de Paul, and—better still!—what Jesus himself experienced and proclaimed, the working masses will recognize Jesus as their brother and Saviour. If the identity of Jesus and the poor, and of the Church and the poor, were explained to them as the mystery of the Real Presence and the Church has been explained, then poor people would feel at home in the Church. Communism draws its strength from a false mystique and dialectic of the proletariat. Only the true mystique and Christian theology of the poor can save humanity from this mirage.

In the light of the Gospel it would then be possible to reconsider methods and techniques which are not entirely traditional, and to consider without fear the apostolate of dedicated priests and laymen living together in small groups, working in order to earn their living, and preaching the Gospel to the poor. This would, of course, require the establishment of training centres for these apostles, and the inauguration of a certain general trend and spirit in the education and training of all priests, since it is in the seminary that those who are called upon to be the models for the flock must first learn to "tend the flocks of God . . . not by constraint, but willingly, not for shameful gain, but eagerly, not as domineering over those in your charge, but being examples to the flock. . . ." (I Peter 5 : 2-3). The servant is not greater than the Master.

Such are the reflections, questions and suggestions which from our vantage point, living and working in Nazareth in the neighbourhood of the carpenter, we have, on the eve of the Council thought it our duty as respectful sons to submit to our bishops, fathers and guardians of our faith in Jesus of Nazareth, pastors of the faithful and apostles to the infidel, and to all those who as theologians and contemplatives are the eyes of the bride of Christ.

III
NAZARETH—PREACHING THE GOSPEL TO THE POOR

Chapter Three
Nazareth—Preaching the Gospel
to the Poor

THE preceding chapter was written for the Fathers of the Council by the fraternities of the Companions of Jesus the Carpenter at the request of their comrades in Nazareth and in collaboration with them.

This final chapter introduces these fraternities to the reader. These cells of the Church, for preaching the Gospel to the poor and to the world of labour, are at once new and very old. They first arose in Nazareth, that small town in modern Israel which, small though it is, on account of the Nazarene still glows with a special effulgence for the modern world. They arose at the time of the Council, in —to use the words of the late Pope John—"this present springtime of the Church".

They are, of course, not the only ones to flourish in our day, the middle of the twentieth century. The germs and beginnings of other movements are also appearing under the influence of the Holy Spirit and in accordance with the apostolic desire of the Church to satisfy the expectation of our modern world, the world of labour and socialization. Without mentioning those congregations of religious whose prayer is at the very heart of the masses, we may congratulate ourselves on the many apostolic secular institutes, including the Worker Mission of SS Peter and Paul, about whose formation we have read in *Journal d'une Mission ouvrière*. Another journal, that of Mgr Ancel, also makes an important contribution to the apostolate amongst the workers. The launching of the worker-priest experiment in France ran into difficulties at first, but it is to be hoped that so much sacrifice and so much goodwill may in the end produce forms of apostolic life which will receive the approval of the hierarchy.

In many countries vocations are seen to be tending towards the preaching of the Gospel to the poor in an apostolic life led in the spirit of the Gospel. On a number of occasions the hierarchy has expressed a desire to encourage such an apostolate. In the meantime the world of working men and poor people is hoping and waiting.

Amongst other such efforts the fraternities also respond to this need and to these vocations in submission to the spirit of Jesus and in all obedience to the hierarchy. Incidentally, they were not formed as the result of any previous plan, but arose as the upshot to a series of encounters in the village of the carpenter.

1. *Nazareth*

"Nazareth is more important than Rome, since without Jesus of Nazareth Rome would be just a capital city like many others." Thus said Doctor Percy, a Jew and Professor at Oxford University. Particularly in times like these, when all eyes are turned towards Rome, it is not a bad thing that someone should re-state this truth. Addressing the fathers of the Council, Jean Farran expressed the same idea in different terms: "You, Most Reverend Fathers, are the Princes of the Church. And yet, Cardinal Ottaviani, your father was a baker. Your father, Cardinal Siri, was a docker. And your father, Mgr Kominek, was a miner in Silesia."

He could have written even more simply: You are all Nazarenes, disciples of Jesus the Carpenter of Nazareth, since "the servant is not greater than the Master".

Nazareth in Former Times

In the course of excavation for the foundations of the new Basilica of the Annunciation, the remains of that small village were uncovered: little dwellings consisting of a room hewn out of the rock, with a small roofing in front, and a baking oven, a cistern and a store-room to one side. There were probably a hundred such hearths in the original village. One of these caves, which, tradition says, was that of Mary, has become the centre of the crypt where the Mystery of the Word made Flesh is venerated. The village itself was built on a hill with a steep drop, the "brow", referred to by Saint Luke (4:29). Near by was a little stream which is now covered over by a street. To the west, amidst tombs and ruins of the first century, the remains of a poor house of two small rooms is venerated as that which belonged to Joseph. There was a fountain there, though it is now dried up, but there is another still working about three hundred yards or so from the old village. A small and very ancient church is called the church of the synagogue and recalls that, in fact, this village was Jewish. Jesus came with Joseph and Mary to pray there and to read the Law and the Prophets. Excavations have turned up potsherds, jugs, an unbroken earthenware pot such as Mary must have used for the kitchen, and the remains of pitchers such as the women still use today to fetch water from the fountain. How one regrets the successive constructions which have covered up what was there before! Erected to the glory of the mystery of the incarnation, they hide the way in which God desired to reveal himself to man, not in human power, but in human poverty—"though he was rich, yet for your sake he became poor, so that through his poverty you might become rich" (II Cor. 8:9). But at least the Gospel itself remains, and in its plain, sober words it tells us enough about the life of the Nazarene to enable us to imagine it in its contemporary context.

Nazareth in our Day

Modern Nazareth provokes more reflection on the mystery of Christ than even the ruins do. Up to 1948 it was a small town of about 12,000 inhabitants, a market centre for the surrounding villages of Galilee, with its souks, its cobblers' and carpenters' workshops, and its donkey market. Then suddenly the Jewish-Arab war caused an influx of refugees into this small and holy place where everyone— Christian, Moslem and Jew—felt safe, as though in the presence of a mother. The little town doubled its population within a week. Families piled in everywhere: into the schools, the Casa Nova, the hovels, the caves, the stables, the henhouses and the pigsties, not to mention the buildings hastily run up to meet the emergency. The churches and the religious communities naturally assisted the refugees most generously. (Incidentally, most of the alms distributed came from Belgium.) But how were all these refugees to be found work and provided with decent lodgings? Never, it seemed, for they waited eight years in misery; and then one day in 1956 there was talk about a workers' city, the Training School of Jesus the Adolescent founded by the Salesian Brothers, and about the "Chicoun" we shall deal with later. The Arab population remained apathetic whilst the Jews flowed into the new Nazareth—"Elit" or the high—built rapidly during the past seven years on one of the ten hills. With its modern blocks of dwelling houses, its shops and its factories, it already has 10,000 inhabitants, and soon it will have 25,000.

Nazareth is a Human Microcosm

Today we can say that Nazareth is a microcosm, a sort of micro-humanity, a place where, on a reduced scale, you meet Arabs and Jews, Easterners and Westerners, rich and

poor, traditional villagers whose roots go back two thou-
sand years, and workers and technicians of the future,
feudalism, liberal employers, trade unionists, co-operatives,
and members of the Histradouth, the powerful working-
class organization that has built up modern Israel.

The various religions also co-exist in Nazareth. There are
12,500 Christians, 12,500 Moslems, and 10,000 Jews. During the day they work side by side as part of the economic
life of the neighbourhood, but they are separate in their
prayers, their traditions and their family life. The three
main Christian groups are each represented amongst the
12,500 Christians: Catholics, Orthodox and Protestants.
There are three Catholic communities: Greek, Latin and
Maronite: and three Orthodox communities: Greek,
Coptic and Armenian. The Protestants are divided into two
main groups: Anglicans and Baptists. But, of course, there
are various other sects as well.

The ecumenical problem presents itself here in terms of
practical personal relations: within the same family there
may be members of different churches. Remembering in
addition the existence of many religious houses—French,
Italian, German and English—you get some idea of how
complex religious life is in present-day Nazareth.

Jesus of Nazareth as seen by Christian, Jew and Moslem

Everyone knows that this city is the home of Jesus of
Nazareth and his mother Mary, but each sees that truth in
his own fashion.

The Christian Nazarenes feel themselves neighbours and
compatriots of Jesus. And the working men of Nazareth,
particularly those in the building trades, regarded themselves as his companions. "What are you trying to tell us?"
demanded Salim, a young Nazarene workman, to Russian
missionaries who wanted to make him acquainted with

a new Gospel. "We know Jesus. He's our neighbour."

The Moslems venerate Jesus as a saint, and his mother Mary as the Immaculate. Those Moslems who live in Nazareth even go farther (though it isn't orthodox on their part!) and venerate her icon and join with the crowd which flocks from church to church on 15 August singing "Holy Mary, protect us!" Some of these Moslems are better versed in the Bible than they are in the Koran and they pray Christian prayers—like Abou Zet, whose entire wealth in his humble room consists of the Koran hung on the wall, and the Bible (both Old and New Testaments) under his pillow within reach of his hand. "In the winter when there's no bread in the house I read the Bible to my wife and children, and it's like butter."

The Jews say least about Jesus and Mary. They clearly feel a little embarrassed—sometimes they are mildly ironic, sometimes openly admiring. Confronted with the Christian presence, meeting Jesus of Nazareth on their return to the land of Abraham, many become thoughtful. One of them said: "Is it true, yes or no, did we crucify Jesus of Nazareth? That's what the Russian Christians say when they want to attack us. But I've never done anything against Jesus." A new Jewish immigrant from Algeria was invited at the Registry Office to change his name, which was Christian, and adopt a Jewish name. But he was very indignant at this and pointing to Nazareth he asked the official: "Where do you people come from? Don't you know this is his country. Jesus the carpenter is over there." Incidentally, this particular Jew was also a carpenter by trade.

The Gospel Message of Nazareth

It was for all these men, to make himself understood by them all, to "make them all rich", that "the Word was made Flesh" and Jesus dwelt amongst them in this place and in his own special manner. Why did he want to be born from the womb of a little Galilean peasant girl? Why did he decide to pass for the son of a carpenter and to work as a village carpenter himself until his thirtieth year?

The mystery of Nazareth is primarily the mystery of the incarnation. The Word was made Flesh here. It is also the mystery of the hidden life of obedience and humility that Jesus led as child and adolescent, upon which Charles de Foucauld in our own day has so profoundly reflected. It is also the mystery of the carpenter, of Jesus the workman, about which people began to speak perhaps not more than fifty years ago, and which has not yet finished casting its light over the world of labour. And, finally, it is the mystery of the anointing and the apostolate for preaching the Gospel to the poor, a primary mystery for the understanding of the episcopate and the apostolate.

Chapter 4 of the Gospel of Saint Luke presents this mystery for the knowledge of faith. At the beginning of his public life Jesus desired to return to Nazareth where he had been brought up, and according to his custom he entered the village synagogue there on the Sabbath day. In this way he underlined the continuity between his apostolic life and his previous life in Nazareth.

Jesus rose to deliver his sermon, and they presented him with the book of the prophet Isaiah, which he opened at the place where it says: "The spirit of the Lord is upon me because he has anointed me to preach good news to the poor." And Jesus declared: "Today this scripture has been fulfilled." The Gospel was preached to the poor of Nazareth by their own carpenter, one of their own people, whose father and mother they knew, and his cousins too, and his trade and his social condition: "Is not this the carpenter, the son of Mary?" (Mark 6:3). Thus the consecrated one, he upon whom the spirit of the Lord rested, he who was sent by his Father, the unique priest, revealed himself in the humble condition of a workman, son of a workman. And so it is today that beyond all the basilicas and other religious buildings which cover Nazareth, both the simple and the more educated people of the city regard the carpenter as having been sent to preach the Gospel to the poor, to staunch wounded hearts, to open the eyes of the blind, to liberate prisoners, and announce the grace of God.

The continuation of the text reveals the extent of Christ's charity. If he entered mankind's laborious condition to that degree it was in order to reach the whole man and all men, the widow of Sarepta and Naaman the Syrian, and not merely an élite, not merely even the chosen people. The conflict had already broken out which was to lead from the brow of the hill at Nazareth to the hill of Golgotha.

The Gospel is not to be enclosed either in the synagogue or the Judeo-Christian church of the early Christian community in Jerusalem. The second Pentecost of Caesarea (Acts 10:44) is already presaged in Jesus' attitude in the synagogue of Nazareth: the Gospel is to be preached to the poor of all races, all nations and all classes.

2. The Companions of Jesus the Carpenter

A few years ago, in about 1954, when the newspapers were busily discussing "the worker-priest affair", a priest, professor at a big seminary, was meditating on this very text, and it seemed to him that he was not living with and for Jesus, at least not socially and in his condition of life. The division between the world of the poor and the Church, like the separation between the Church and the world of labour, seemed to him to be a "schism", a wound in the body of Christ, because Christ is identified both with the

Church and with the poor. Rightfully therefore the Church should primarily be "the Church of the poor".

To communicate with Jesus in his working members this priest asked for and obtained from his bishop permission to live and work as a workman amongst workmen. He felt that Nazareth, in modern, socially advanced Israel, would be a privileged place in which to extend the spiritual basis of an apostolic life spent in a working class environment in order to preach the Gospel to the poor and to establish the Church in the world of labour. The Melkite Archbishop of Galilee, Mgr George Hakim, invited him to come to his diocese. Before long this priest was joined by young people who had heard the same appeal to live a life consecrated to preaching the Gospel to the poor. In this way the Fraternity of the *Companions of Jesus the Carpenter* was founded, or, as they are called in short: the Companions of Nazareth. A similar body for women, with the same name, was also founded there.

Their Spirit and their Training[1]

With the approval of Mgr Hakim and of a number of other bishops who wish to have them in their dioceses, these Fraternities aspire to live in the Church in accordance with the prophecy of Isaiah that Jesus fulfilled in himself: "The spirit of the Lord God is upon me" (Isaiah 51 : 1). This consecration, Christ's mission, is prolonged in the episcopate, the source of all benediction and apostolate. Thus the Companions ask the episcopate to bless them and to send them out "to preach the Gospel to the poor", to give them that Nazarene oil of the Spirit. In practice the Companions live and work with the labouring masses in the world of labour, and in particular amongst peoples who are not yet Catholic, or who have been de-christianized, in the

[1] Cf. the Proposed Way of Life for the Companions of Jesus, pp. 123ff., below.

4

under-developed countries or in those countries which are a prey to atheism. The central mystery which supports their life of faith is the contemplation of Jesus the carpenter of Nazareth, living still as always in his Church and also in the poor, his favourite members. Their life is nourished and sustained by the reading of the Gospel and the Bible. They live the life of workers in small Fraternities of two or three, in prayer, chastity, obedience to the Church and a life of labour. At present their main training centre is in Nazareth.

For the first year candidates work the eight hours of their employment, at whatever job it may be, but are given no apostolic or social charge, in order that they may prepare themselves morally, spiritually and intellectually. During the second year they do not have a job, in order to be able to devote themselves entirely to the Gospel and to the spiritual life in a kind of novitiate, whilst still remaining close to their Fraternity. After this they resume the normal life of a worker.

Their closer association with the Church takes place in the various stages which Jesus laid down for his own apostles:

Invitation: "Come and see"

Call: "Come and I will make you fishers of men"

Nomination: "He declares them apostles"

Consecration: "The spirit of the Lord is upon me"

Apostolate: "As my Father sent me so also do I send you"

The bishop supervises these stages, thus conferring grace and mission. This formation leads to the apostolic life, and fulfils itself within the framework and the spirit of this life. For those who are already priests, this training is shortened and adapted. Those who intend to become priests take the normal training course.

The Apostolate

This apostolate is not an action, not a work, not a mingling of contemplation and action. It is not a question of "doing an apostolic thing". In modern times the apostolate has been reduced to certain of the secondary forms of Catholic action, charitable works, teaching, social action, lay movements. . . . This conception explains why some people fight shy of any active apostolates in an organized form. In reality, according to the Gospel and the Acts of the Apostles, to be an apostle is to take part in the life of Jesus, the representative of the Father, who prolongs his mission in the Church by means of the apostles and their collaborators. Today the apostle is first of all the bishop, the successor of the apostles, consecrated and sent to preach the Gospel to the poor. The bishop is he who disseminates the word of truth, the Gospel of salvation, and who presides at prayer. Thus understood, the apostolate is a close fusion of prayer and the ministry of the Word. This presupposes truly apostolic prayer and a ministry of the Word which is truly prayer. This ministry of the Word is primarily addressed to the poor, who are so often neglected to the advantage of the rich—to the people outside the church, to the dechristianized masses, to our separated brethren.

This ministry of the Word begins with a life which truly and visibly conforms with the Gospel. It is also the Word properly so called—conversations, chats, articles, films, etc. . . . depending on what openings there are. Jesus accompanied his ministry of the Word with miracles and signs of his goodness. And he continued to confirm the Word of the apostles by signs of charity which were no longer miracles and yet nevertheless were often unexpected fruits of the Word. The Word and prayer thus tend to express themselves in various kinds of social action according to circumstances. Without ever involving themselves in the sense of temporal works or organizations the Companions share by the ministry of the Word in the working-class movement for social justice and for the advancement of the poor towards a materially better life. According to circumstances they will promote or encourage whatever seems suitable out of a practical love for Jesus living in his members: "I was hungry and you gave me to eat." Neither benevolent condescension nor a passive sharing of their life are enough. At all times, in season and out of season, the sword of the Word must be used to shake up and awaken the rich and powerful and to encourage the poor. And finally, the Companions take part to whatever extent is possible in the ecumenical movement, since unbelievers cannot believe if Christians are not visibly one in Jesus.

Such, in broad outline, is the apostolic life of the Companions of the Carpenter. During recent years other movements, within families, groups or secular institutes, have formed themselves in the Church in reply to the expectation of a world which says, as the Macedonian said to Paul: "Come with us." There are many vocations with this emphasis. It is to be hoped that the Council will confirm and encourage this movement of the Spirit. Incidentally, there is nothing new in it, nothing modern. This life is as traditional in the Church as the Acts of the Apostles or the Gospel. The women Companions desire no more than to live as Mary of Nazareth and Mary Magdalene lived; and the men desire no more than to live as Philip, Paul, Stephen and the other first Companions of the Gospel lived.

3. Two Complementary Apostolic Experiments

This apostolic life has already been lived by the Companions in a variety of very different circles in Nazareth. As we have already seen, this city presents in miniature a picture of the outside world in its most varied aspects. In addition it is situated within the territory of the new State of Israel, a veritable laboratory of social experiments—from the agricultural kibbutz to the big neo-capitalist factory. This background is very valuable for our social training, but it is no more than a starting point for the Companions; a providential one perhaps, but not in any way definitive. The Companions are "Nazarenes", but not in the sense that they are restricted to Nazareth, or even Israel, and must remain there always. However, this particular location does allow them two forms of apostolic presence which are complementary and highly illuminating.

(a) *The co-operatives of Nazareth*

In Nazareth, first of all, they have been, from the very beginning, amongst a mixed population of Arabs, Christians and Moslems. As we have already seen, the Jewish-Arab war of 1948 produced a great influx of refugees, and apart from a few rich people who were either indifferent to their needs or actively exploiting them, these masses have vegetated in misery. Of course there are schools and hospitals, in which Catholic or Protestant missionaries work with admirable devotion. The bare necessities of food and clothing have been distributed.

However, as in most countries where similar misery reigns, there has been no fundamental remedy, and no real attempt to get to the root of the matter: the unhygienic living conditions and the insecurity and irregularity of employment. One working-class family out of three lives with its seven or eight members in conditions often unworthy of human beings and always unhygienic, with the walls sweating with damp or running with infected water. The ikons and crucifixes hanging on the walls are often besmirched by water dripping from the cesspits of the houses built in terraces above. One family lives in a

cave without light and almost without air, with the result
that its children are half-blind. . . . One workman in three
is in a state of chronic unemployment, which is the main
cause of misery and wretchedness in Nazareth. It was because he lived in such conditions that Abou Said, the father
of seven children went off his head and abandoned his wife
and children, although he loved them deeply. Before this
happened he had already refused alms, saying: "I don't
want charity. I want work so that I can feed my family."
This is the sort of thing that opened the eyes of the first
Companions. Could they stop short at sharing a life of
misery and labour with their comrades?

Ought they not to speak, *to proclaim the Gospel*? "Let
he who has two coats give one to him who has none. . . .
Love one another. . . . I was hungry and you gave me to
eat."

They formed a group of workmen and with their help
conducted an investigation into conditions of work and
housing in three different quarters, embracing some two
hundred families. On the basis of their results they now
drew up a report—"*S.O.S. Nazareth!*"—which they sub-
mitted to the proper ecclesiastical, governmental and trade
union authorities, with the encouragement of Mgr Hakim
and other church leaders. They met with understanding
and sympathy from trade union and government officials,
who all did what they could, but they came up against a
wall of suspicion on the part of the very people they were
anxious to help. However, they formed a group of thirteen
people who needed work and a place for their families to
live, and with them founded the first co-operative, a social
form which is highly developed in Israel. This they named
Chicoun, the house. The fact that a priest was amongst
them gave the members of this first co-operative confidence
and courage, and renewed their belief in society, in themselves, and in God and his Church, which now no longer

appeared to them as for the rich only—not even for those rich who were generous with their alms—but as "the Church of the poor", both a mother and a sister.

Unfortunately, however, the very poor could not join the new co-operative because the members had to raise two-fifths of the initial starting capital—the Government and the trade unions between them provided the other three-fifths. But those people who were forced by this necessity to stay outside were precisely the people whose need for work and a roof over their heads was greatest of all!

A Belgian priest, the Abbé Warlomont, the Vicar of Saint Jacques in Tournai, happened to be on a pilgrimage to Nazareth at the time, and whilst he was there he came to hear about this co-operative and its difficulties, and made the acquaintance of the priest who was one of its members. The result was that the Abbé no longer looked at Nazareth merely with the eyes of a pilgrim to the Holy Places. As a pilgrim of the body of Christ he saw that its most beloved members were rotting in tumble-down hovels. It was his encounter in faith with Jesus the carpenter. On his return to his own country he publicized the great need and sold his own car to buy the co-operative *Chicoun* a concrete mixer. After this it was not long before money began pouring through his letter box for the cause. The movement had been well and truly launched, and thanks to the aid it was able to supply it proved possible to grant long-term loans without, or almost without, interest to the families in greatest need. In addition to *Chicoun* there is now another housing co-operative *Aroué* (i.e. the brothers). Together they embrace 180 families, 160 of whom have already been re-housed; the remainder should have been re-housed by March 1963. Of these 180 families, thirty-one had nothing to bring into the co-operative but their own poverty, and twenty others were unable to raise more than the half, and sometimes even only a quarter, of their share capital.

By means of weekly payments all these families are now gradually becoming the owners of their own houses and gardens.

In order to build the houses in the first place it became necessary to found a *building co-operative* as distinct from the housing co-operative. This building co-operative works at the lowest possible rates and, in particular, it reinforces the local struggle to compel all employers to respect social justice in the matter of wages, social insurance, permanent employment and so on. The great volume of wretchedness and misery in many countries is often largely due to a lack of social justice and effective working-class organization. This was the case in Nazareth. The rich enriched themselves at the cost of the poor, who were a source of cheap labour. What a misfortune it was for the Church to seem to be on the side of the rich, who were in fact even making a profit from the Church! Nazareth could not be allowed to remain in a state of paternalism and feudalism in a country like Israel, which had set up a sound social organization inspired by the spirit of the prophets.

The Companions have also assisted in the founding of another co-operative, this time for dressmaking and embroidery, and known as *Tabitha*. Thanks to this co-operative the local sempstresses are able to fight against their exploitation by the wholesalers, who pay low rates for their labour and sometimes even palm worthless cheques onto them. The members of *Tabitha* now sew and embroider and sell their production on their own account, and in this way the economic position of women in Nazareth is improving. At the same time these Arab women, who are still relegated to the interior of their houses, come to share in social progress. Altogether it is a new resurrection—hence the name *Tabitha*, or Dorcas the sempstress, a woman full of good works, who was brought back to life by St Peter (Acts 9:36).

These co-operatives are supported and assisted by a movement of fraternal solidarity which began in Tournai and spread first to Bastogne and the Flemish areas, and subsequently to France (Paris, Dijon, Pau, Bordeaux, Lyons), Germany, Switzerland and the United States. It now became necessary to give this movement a definite organizational form. This led to the founding of the *"Amos" Fraternity*, Amos being the proletarian prophet of the God of the poor and of social justice. This organization collects the gifts and turns them into long-term loans. Subsequently such funds can be applied elsewhere. A further great advantage of this arrangement is that the poor do not feel humiliated by gifts, or under any particular obligation to their benefactors. They take a normal place in the social and economic system, have their own accounts at the Workers Bank, and so on.

Having done so much for Nazareth, in January 1963 the friends of the Amos Fraternity were invited to continue their work, not in Nazareth this time, but in Bethlehem, where there was a great deal of want. "Do not ornament the churches if it means neglecting your brother, since this temple is more important than that" (Saint John Chrysostom). But twenty families were huddled in caves around the Grotto of the Nativity, which has become a gilded crypt of the Imperial Basilica. Last Christmas a baby died of malnutrition in one of those caves. Its name was Aissa (Jesus), and its mother's name was Mary. Why not do in Bethlehem what had been done in Nazareth? After all, in Nazareth they had also said: "The thing's impossible. That priest's mad. Nothing will come of it." But all things are possible when the Word of God is taken seriously. In Rome it is being said that many bishops (those who have not already done so) are anxious to give their cross of gold and their ring so that Christ may be housed in Bethlehem.[1]

So the Companions of Jesus the Carpenter have their first training centre in the workers' city of Nazareth. One of them works as a member of the building co-operative which is building this city. Their training is taking place in completely working-class surroundings both for work and for living. They have decided not to accept housing in permanent buildings, and are content to live in huts. "We have no children," they say. "We will accept proper housing when all those workmen with families have been re-housed." Their chapel is in a cave which was once the home of a family, exactly like that in that old village where "He dwelt amongst us." But this one is intact. There is even a crypt in it and this has been made into a tabernacle. The Fraternity brethren gather here for Holy Communion.

The women Companions have a training centre in Bethlehem, and the two communities have other centres in view for the future, one in Jerusalem, and another on the shore of the Lake, in order to be able to live the Gospel in the Holy Places themselves. However, they are not in the least restricted to these places, and they are prepared to "go and preach to all nations, to the ends of the earth", to go everywhere and anywhere Jesus sends them.

(b) *In the kibbutz, a valuable lesson for the apostolate*

They have already been called upon to live and work in conditions altogether different from those in the workers' city of Nazareth. Some of them have worked in factories,

[1] Those who feel inclined to take part in the movement should get into touch with the Abbé Warlomont at Tournai in Belgium, specifying "Amos". They will receive the Bulletin *"Vers Nazareth-Bethléem"*. In France, Grappin, 5 rue Cap. Giraud, Talaud (Côte-d'Or), Dijon 445-19.

in hotels and, above all, in kibbutzim collective farms, and in particular in the kibbutz of Ginossar on the shore of the lake in the plain of Genesareth. It is a real privilege to be able to live in such a neighbourhood, to sail as a fisherman on the lake, to repair the nets on land, and so on.

This kibbutz heard of the companions' manner of life and invited one fraternity of the men Companions and one of the women Companions to come to the kibbutz and work there for a minimum period of six months. The invitation was accepted, and a number of other Christian men and women joined the Companions. The kibbutz organized an *oulpan* (an intensive course of Hebrew) for them, and put a room at their disposal as a chapel. Those who took part in the experiment lived and worked in great amity with the original members of the kibbutz, despite the fact that the ideology of this kibbutz, as of most kibbutzim, is marxist, though each member is left free to hold his own personal opinions. Right from the beginning relationships were very frank and objective, and living and working together in a community helped to clear up a good many prejudices and misunderstandings, and generally made for better relations between Christian and Jew. Without making any concessions at all in the matter of doctrine it proved possible to arrive at such a degree of mutual understanding and mutual esteem that the kibbutz invited a fraternity, dedicated priests and laymen, to come to the kibbutz again and remain in the community. This, of course, would prove difficult on account of the pressure the collective exerts on the individual, but from the apostolic point of view how could one possibly ignore this invitation of the modern Macedonians? Their aim was not to recruit for marxism, but to contribute to mutual understanding.

A good many members of these kibbutzim have now pretty thoroughly applied zionism and marxism with very satisfactory practical results. But all the same they are not completely content with their achievements, since they can see that no matter how perfect the terrestrial city may become it can never exhaust or satisfy all man's possibilities. There is something else, there is another hope. Some of them look towards the Church, but the Church seems so very far away from them. Apart from the resentment the Jewish people feel towards the Christian world, they are even more conscious of the apprehension that the socialist world, which wants its social order to be homogeneous and perfect, feels towards that other, capitalist world, as though the Church were bound up with that form of pseudo-civilization which they have had the courage to leave behind.

The kibbutz with its two characteristics—labour and community—is a typical modern organism. In order to live in a kibbutz you must work like everyone else in the place decided on by the community. This is the same situation as exists in the communist world, which embraces about two-thirds of all humanity today. If we are to preach the Gospel to this world then we must accept a common language, the "nationality" created by manual or technical labour and socialization. Of these two elements, the first, labour, contains nothing which is contrary either to the Gospel or the Church; it only does so if it is turned into a god, a state of affairs which is fortunately true of only a few fanatical members of the kibbutzim. However, in order to save these men and this form of social life by adding a Gospel leaven, first we must at least accept that form of "socialization" recommended by Pope John XXIII in *Mater et Magistra*. The apostles working in this particular world must act in accordance with the instructions issued to missionaries. There is, incidentally, nothing at all "progressive" or "modern" about these instructions, since they were issued for the Propagation of the Faith as long ago as 1659.

"Be not overzealous, and advance no arguments designed to persuade these peoples to change their rites, their customs and their morals, unless they are obviously contrary to religion and true morality. What could be more absurd than to attempt to transfer the customs of France, Spain and Italy, or of any other European country, to the Chinese? Your task is not to introduce your countries to these peoples, but our faith, which neither rejects nor offends the rites and customs of any people, provided that such rites and customs are not of themselves detestable. On the contrary, it is anxious to preserve them. It is, so to speak, rooted in the nature of man to love his own country and its traditions, and to place them above all others in the world. Thus one of the most frequent and lively causes of estrangement and hatred is the attempt to make changes in the customs proper to a nation, and in particular in those which have been practised from time immemorial. What would happen if, having abrogated such customs, you replaced them by the customs of your own country, imposed on a strange people from without? Never compare the customs of these peoples with the customs of the peoples of Europe. On the contrary, do your best to get used to strange customs, and admire and praise anything that is worthy of admiration and praise in them. Where such customs are not admirable you will not praise them fulsomely as flatterers do, but you will be prudent enough to reserve your judgement; at the very least you will not condemn them vehemently and to excess. As for those customs which are quite definitely bad, you must discredit them more by shaking your head sorrowfully, or by your disapproving silence, than by condemning them in words, without, of course, neglecting those opportunities when, once souls are inclined to embrace the truth, such customs may be uprooted without fuss."

Thus on the whole all that need be done there is to do as Jesus did in Nazareth: to work, and to live the social life of the village whilst extending it in the apostolate. These communities—and in this respect too they are once again typical of modern society—do not need the schools, dispensaries and churches that the Church often provides as part of her work to obtain a foothold in a community. Such communities already have their schools, their dispensaries and their Houses of Culture, and so far they do not feel the need for churches. The apostolate must therefore start at the beginning, with a humble, patient and saving presence, a solidarity in labour, and all else "excluding sin", the bearing of witness to a charity stronger and more profound than socialist solidarity.

To approach these new poor in a new world—materially prosperous, but poor in the essential things—we need have nothing and bring nothing with us but two hands with which to labour, and a heart sustained by the Gospel with which to love.

Whilst working as fishermen on the lake of Genesareth and drawing in their nets as Simon Peter, Andrew, James and John did before them, the Companions were thinking of the successor of Peter at the helm of the Church, and of the bishops, "the fishers of men". One day one of the Companions whose job it was to repair the nets wrote a deeply filial letter to Pope John. He and his fellow Christian Companions were rewarded with a personal reply and an apostolic benediction. The comrades of the kibbutz felt that they too had been blessed and they were overjoyed. "Thank Pope John," they said, and then they asked: "Is he going to free the Church from its compromising relationship with wealth? We Jews ceased to be the chosen people because we loved money too much. You can't serve both God and mammon. Here in our kibbutz we have removed money from our personal preoccupations. Can't the Church liberate herself from money too? Is the Church allied with the rich? Jesus himself was a poor man amongst poor men."

It was talk such as this, heard day after day from both Jews and Arabs in circumstances in which the need for the Gospel grows continuously that persuaded the Companions of Jesus to write the memorandum "Jesus, the Church and the Poor" for their Archbishop Mgr Hakim, which is printed as Part II of this book.[1]

At first the Archbishop was taken by surprise, then he re-read the memorandum, and finally he said: "A copy of this must be placed in the hands of all the fathers of the Council. Come with me to the Council." Mgr Himmer, the Bishop of Tournai, who is himself greatly exercised by the loss of faith amongst the working men of the mining and industrial district that comprises his diocese, and who, through the Abbé Warlomont, follows our efforts in Nazareth, also encouraged the distribution of this brochure. At his invitation and that of Mgr Hakim, more and more bishops came together, all of them deeply interested in these questions. Amongst them was Mgr Mercier, the Bishop of the Shara, a very large diocese (three times as big as Spain) in which there is great destitution and endemic famine, side by side with great wealth from oil deposits. Cardinal Gerlier and the Patriarch Maximos joined with the bishops in supporting this appeal. "Divine grace is working in the hearts of the bishops," as one of them said. In fact a profound movement is at work, brought about by the meeting of bishops from Chile, Japan, Italy, Belgium and India, who have already adopted important decisions so that the Church may have the appearance of being most certainly the Church of all men, but most particularly the Church of the poor. However, they acted and spoke on their own, and sometimes they were

[1] Pp. 55-86 above.

adversely criticized by their followers. They met together
in Rome, aware that the same spirit animates the whole
Church in face of the great questions :

How can the Gospel be preached to the poor?

How can we give back to the Church her real features,
those of Jesus the carpenter?

How can the Gospel be preached to the rich so that they
will consent to share their riches with the poor?

How can we help to equip those countries which are
still under-developed?

How can the Church be established in the world of
labour and socialization?

All these questions, which are closely connected, "do not
seem to have been expressly and specifically provided for
in the programme of the Council," as Cardinal Gerlier
pointed out. "But nevertheless," he continued, "unless we
tackle them we shall be avoiding the most topical aspects
of evangelical and human reality. It is necessary that this
question should be discussed, and we should insist that
those responsible should raise it. There is a danger that
everything else may remain ineffectual if this question is
not raised and discussed. It is essential that the Church,
which has no desire to be rich, should be saved from the
appearance of riches. It is essential that the Church should
appear as she really is : the mother of the poor, primarily
interested in providing her children with bread for both
body and soul. As Pope John XXIII himself declared on
1 September 1962 : 'The Church is and wishes to be
the Church of all, but in particular the Church of the
poor.'

"The Church must guide those who have what is
materially necessary for life towards the realization that
they must provide them for those who still lack them. We
must see to it, bishops, that the problem of preaching the
Gospel to the poor, and the apostolate amongst working

people, is placed in the centre of our conciliary affairs. The present Council should be used as an opportunity for underlining this. I am personally going to try to speak to everyone willing to listen about this matter."

The Patriarch Maximos declared: "There are two big matters with which the Council must deal: the unity of Christendom and the preaching of the Gospel to the poor, and these two questions are related. It is not so much a question of rich and poor as it is a question of the working people, who represent the vital force of the present-day world."

Mgr Helder Camera (of Rio de Janeiro, the bishop whose diocese contains those "favellas" we have mentioned)[1] proposed that after the Council there should be a meeting under the auspices of the Pope between such bishops as were interested and a certain number of technical experts from the world in course of development. Everyone insisted that the Council should speedily turn to these questions, either by the formation of a special secretariat for the preaching of the Gospel to the poor and for questions *ad extra*, i.e., exterior to the Church and concerning her relations with the outside world, or by dealing with these questions as part of the study of the schema relating to the Church herself, which was just beginning. Cardinal Montini and Cardinal Suenens, following a number of other bishops, intervened during the session to raise these points. Patriarch Maximos felt able to say: "Even if there is no immediate practical result, the seed has been sown, and it will grow and bear fruit." The Companions who, amongst others, put these same questions to the fathers of the Council, were like the child that Jesus placed one day in the middle of his disciples. Thanks to the meeting of all the bishops troubled by the physical and moral misery of their people, the Council has been brought to consider, as Pope John XXIII

[1] cf. p. 27 above.

exhorted, the practical implications of the immense harvest
awaiting the sickle. "Lift up your eyes, and see how the
fields are already white for the harvest" (John 4:35).

CONCLUSION

Conclusion

On 8 December 1962, the feast day of the Immaculate Mary of Nazareth, the day the first session of the Vatican Council ended, there was great joy amongst those who were awaiting a reply to the questions put by the poor and the workers of the whole world to the fathers of the Council. The reports of the 35th general session appeared in the press and particularly in *La Croix*. Under the heading "The Council has found the Right Path", Antoine Wenger reported the intervention of Cardinal Lercaro, Archbishop of Bologna in Italy:

" 'The Pope has taken all necessary steps to ensure the continuation of the business of the Council in the spirit set out in the opening discourse, which won the support of the immense majority of the fathers.

"Let us recall in a few words just what that spirit was. It is not a question of formulating any ancient doctrine anew. What has already been done has been well done. The Church must now be presented to the men and women of our day in a language they can understand, a language which will enable them to accept the message of the Mother Church. The Church must also be presented as the community of all men saved by Jesus Christ but of the poor in particular, those who sometimes find themselves really and truly rejected even by the Church, and almost always find themselves so rejected in appearance.

"The Council will speak in a universal language, and this language will adopt certain accents. During Friday's session Cardinal Lercaro particularly stressed one such accent he regarded as necessary: the life and the actions of the Church should be marked by the accent of poverty. Poverty is the sign of the incarnation. The prophets who announced its coming, the Virgin Mary who was its instrument, and Bethlehem, the place where it came about, were all marked by the sign of poverty. But our modern world insults the poverty of two-thirds of mankind. The Council cannot evade the question raised for the Church by these thousands of millions of poor people. It is therefore desirable that the schema relating to the Church should set out the doctrine of poverty of and in the Church, and underline the eminent dignity of the poor in whom God hides his glory. At the same time it should reveal the connection between the presence of Christ in the poor and his action in the eucharist and in the hierarchy.

"It should certainly go forward with wisdom and prudence in carrying out this reform, but at the same time without fear and without compromise. In consequence it will be necessary to define the use of material wealth in the Church in such a way that the Church will always be able to say as Peter and John said: 'Gold and silver have I none, but what I have I give you.' Let the bishops, many of whom really are poor, truly look as if they are poor, for fear of scandalizing the poor. Let there be real sacerdotal poverty, a poverty like that of the religious congregations who are vowed to poverty. If the Church is true to her poverty then she will find illumination in her poverty, and she will devise the most suitable way of preaching the whole Gospel, the message of God, who for the love of us all made himself poor, though he was rich.

"Loud applause greeted the intervention of Cardinal Lercaro.

"We may compare his intervention with that of Cardinal Suenens and Cardinal Montini. Thus the breach has been made to clear the way for the Council, or rather the way along which the work of the Council must proceed.

"Despite the absence of spectacular results, the first session of the Council has certainly not worked in vain. Those who from the beginning were witnesses of its first gropings, its inquiries and its difficulties are now filled with amazement to observe what the Holy Spirit has brought about through the medium of human discussion. As on the first day so we say again on this last day: 'Confirma hoc Deus'. Confirm, O God, that which thou has brought in us in your holy temple of Jerusalem, that Jerusalem represented in all truth by the Second Vatican Council."

At the end of this same 35th general session Mgr Hakim rose, as Bishop of Galilee, to express the same wish:

"The Pope has certainly opened up a new path which corresponds to the aspirations of the world, the world which St Paul said was suffering the pangs of birth, the world which hopes that the Church will be its universal mother, 'the Church of all, but particularly the Church of the poor' as the Holy Father himself said on 11 September last, and as Cardinal Lercaro has just reminded us in such moving terms.

"It is certain that the true results of our Council will not make themselves felt for ten or fifteen years. What will the world be like then? What will the Church be like then? Whether it wants to or not, a Council at the end of the twentieth century must be a Council for the twenty-first century, when humanity will have doubled in numbers and reached the six milliard mark, and when hunger will be twice as widespread too. What will be the position of the Gospel in the world then?

"This is why we should like to find in the schema of the Church not so much the text of the classic manuals of the past, exact though they may have been, but rather what the world of tomorrow will expect of us. We must demand that the world be addressed in the language of our own century, and that the Second Vatican Council shall do for the episcopate what the First Vatican Council did for the papacy; that, in short, we should speak as Pope John XXIII speaks and as the Gospel speaks. It would be so comforting to speak of the Church as '*Mater amabilis*', and of the papal primacy, or of episcopal power, as a state of service, as a reply to the question of the Lord: 'Peter, do you love me more than these?' Such language would be understood by all, Christians and non-Christians alike."

It now remains for us to pray that the words will be followed by action, because as the first verse of the first chapter of the Acts of the Apostles tells us: "Jesus began to do and teach." And as St Mark tells us, he continued to act with his apostles, confirming the Word by the signs which accompanied it.

Hearing what was done at the Council, and how more and more bishops had taken up the message they had addressed to it, the working people of Nazareth reacted in typically Gospel fashion. One woman exclaimed: "I would like to hug those bishops!" And someone else exclaimed: "Splendid! Let them go on and really do something now."

APPENDIX I

PROPOSED WAY OF LIFE FOR THE COMPANIONS OF JESUS OF NAZARETH THE CARPENTER

Appendix I
Proposed Way of Life for the Companions of Jesus of Nazareth the Carpenter

Note: the word "proposed" does not signify a programme which has yet to be carried out, because, in fact, several Fraternities of the Companions have already been living along such lines for four years before ever it was drawn up. It is a form, a rule, a way of life. But as the only real rule of life is that of the Gospel the proposals have necessarily to be reviewed from time to time, whereas the Gospel itself is always before us as the true rule of life.

The Fraternity of the Companions of Jesus of Nazareth the Carpenter, is a society of Christians within the Catholic Church completely dedicated to Jesus of Nazareth and to the preaching of the Gospel to the poor.

I. THE AIM OF THE COMPANIONS

Its aim is to live the Gospel in the light of that verse of Luke 4 proceeding from Isaiah 51 in which Jesus reveals his messianic consecration and his mission to preach the Gospel to the poor in the context of his own life as a carpenter in Nazareth. The Companions live this life of Jesus in his social condition as a carpenter, receiving from the Church a share of his dedication and his mission to preach the Gospel to the poor. As Nazarenes they live the apostolic life of Jesus, ready to go with him to Jerusalem in the hope of the resurrection.

In practice we live and labour with the poor, with the labouring masses, with the world of labour and, above all, with those who are not yet Catholic, or who have been de-christianized, and in the under-developed countries, or in those countries which are a prey to atheism. But by faith, hope and love we see Jesus of Nazareth in them, and it is with him that we live and work.

II. THE MYSTERY OF JESUS TO WHOM WE ARE DEDICATED AS SERVANTS AND WITNESSES

Following the example of Paul on the way to Damascus we contemplate Jesus resurrected and living in his Church (Acts 26:16). At the same time we contemplate him in his favourite members, the poor (Matt. 25:31).

1. *Jesus of Nazareth the Carpenter*

The Companions of Jesus of Nazareth contemplate Christ glorious, commune with his love, revering "the blessed and venerable hands" of the carpenter. In his unique act of Redemption Jesus remains for ever what he was here below for the salvation of all men in all ages. Of all the stages in his life on earth that during which he was a carpenter in the village of Nazareth was the longest. This mystery can enlighten present-day humanity in its consciousness of labour and the human community. Amongst all the states of life Jesus chose this one as that most suited to the redemption of the world. We live with him as he lived.

The apostolic life of Jesus is linked with Nazareth, where he decided to inaugurate it by reading Isaiah 61 in his village synagogue (Luke 4:16). He wished to be known as a carpenter and as the son of a carpenter. All his preaching is that of a working man talking of the things he knows; the sower, the reaper, the woman preparing the food. Right up to the last, in his Passion, he remained the prophet of Galilee, and on the cross he was "Jesus of Nazareth". The Word was made flesh and dwelt amongst us even to this extent.

2. *Jesus Living in his Church*

Jesus of Nazareth continues to live with us here below in his Church as he revealed to Paul: "I am Jesus whom you are persecuting." The doctrine which is today called the Mystical Body is at the heart of all apostolic life. This vision sustains the apostle and enables him to accomplish in his flesh that which is missing in the Passion of Christ for the sake of his body which is the Church.

We have the same love for Jesus of Nazareth and for his Church, the real, hierarchical, sacramental, human and divine Church. "Christ and the Church are one." And we can love him and serve him only in communion with the Church, one, holy, catholic and apostolic.

The same love and the same tenderness turn us towards Jesus of Nazareth and his Vicar on earth, Bishop of Rome, towards Jesus of Nazareth and his bishops, successors of his apostles, heads of the apostolate. Sacramentally and collegially with Peter, they are the "gentle Christ on earth", "pastors with the chief of pastors".

The apostle is moved by a faith which is lucid, enlightened, courageous, humble, filial and loving in this mystery of the Church, and which preserves him in the way of truth. The Companions of Jesus the Carpenter study and pray this doctrine. They keep close filial contact with the episcopate on which they depend and from which they receive their apostolate. They work closely together with it in order that the cell of the Church they represent, and the Church as a whole, shall "reproduce the image of Christ—which is Jesus of Nazareth, the Carpenter—in all possible perfection in her whole mode of life, both visible and invisible" (*Mystici Corporis*).

3. *Jesus Living in the Poor, his Best-loved Members*

As Jesus is identified in a certain way with his Church and lives mysteriously in her, so also is he identified by a certain love for the poor, in whom he also lives mysteriously. Not only was he born and died in poverty; not only did he desire of his own will to live and work as a carpenter, but also he affirmed his identity with those who are hungry, with those who go in rags, with those who have no roof over their heads . . . with the poor and those who labour (Matt. 25:31; Luke 16:19; James 2:1-7; 5:1-9). A whole spiritual tradition stems from this mysterious identification of Jesus with the poor. We want to live that love, recognizing and loving by faith Jesus in his labouring members, and living in a real communion with him through them.

The poor are not only those who find it difficult to obtain the material necessities of life, they are also those who have not yet received the light of Christ, the "godless", those without hope in this world, the lost sheep, the prodigal sons, all who have strayed and are not yet saved. All those people outside the Church, both in the East and in the West, those despised ones whom no one thinks of inviting to the feast —they are the first to whom we are sent by the apostolic love of Jesus. "If you love me, *feed my* lambs, feed my sheep. . . ." (not "*direct thy* sheep"). Today it is primarily towards the East that the Light should shine, and the Eastern Churches are best placed to preach the Gospel in that quarter. Thus, without abandoning the West, the Com-

panions turn towards the East, placing themselves for preference in the service of the Eastern Churches, encouraged
by the words of Pope John XXIII: "You who have turned
towards the East, you who have placed yourself under the
jurisdiction of that Eastern bishop, I congratulate,
encourage and bless you. We need to turn in that
direction."

4. One Love, One Christ, One Church

Jesus of Nazareth lives on in his Church which is one
and must appear as one in order that the world may believe
that the Father has sent his Son (John 17:21). Thus the
Companions love all who have been baptized, and in
accordance with their opportunities and the instructions of
their bishops they work for Christian unity and the
ecumenical movement.

But beyond the schism of the churches they are keenly
aware of that other schism, that gap, albeit only
apparent, between the hierarchical Church, the body of
Christ, and the poor, the eminent members of Jesus
Christ. Thus, entirely faithful to the hierarchical Church
and socially integrated with the poor, the Companions will
contribute according to their powers and to the mission they
have received from the Church, to making visible the profound unity of the Church and of the poor in Jesus
of Nazareth, the Carpenter, the head of the body.

III. WHAT MANNER OF SPIRIT ARE YOU OF?

When his disciples James and John desired him to command fire to come down from heaven to consume the un-
believing villages, Jesus replied: "You do not know
what manner of spirit you are of. For the Son of man came
not to destroy men's lives, but to save them" (Luke 9:55-6).

And again: "The Son of man came not to be served, but to serve" (Matt. 20 : 28).

The Companions of the Nazarene are dedicated to Jesus the carpenter, apostle and saviour, sent to preach the Gospel to the poor, striving in the first place to convert themselves to the Gospel, to accept the Gospel themselves, to live in the spirit of Jesus, meditating for choice on those texts in which this spirit is manifest, and applying them in their own practical life.

They read and accept these texts with realism and simplicity, without much commentary and without idealization, but applying them directly; not as the scribes and the doctors did, but as Jesus did, seeing him always through and beyond the texts. They join with the apostles and disciples, with Mary and the holy women, and they allow themselves to be guided by their example in the spirit which is "the soul of the Church" (Pius XII, *Mystici Corporis*) and in all obedience to the hierarchical Church, mother and mistress of holiness and the apostolate.

Luke 4 : 14-30. The main text. Jesus reveals himself, after Isaiah 61, as the dedicated one, sent by the Father to preach the Gospel to the poor—and nevertheless he remained Jesus of Nazareth, the carpenter. He announced that the good tidings would be addressed to those outside the chosen race. And they sought to kill him. . . . But he passed through their midst as he would later pass through death to his Father to send the spirit to the Church so that the Gospel might be preached to all peoples.

Thus the Companions ask the Church to give them the consecrating spirit of Jesus, and to be sent to preach the Gospel to the poor, to those outside, whilst themselves remaining poor, working men with the carpenter, accepting the cross which this involves, and whatever cross he may see fit to impose upon them, including martyrdom itself if that should please him.

Isaiah 61 which Jesus willed to read and applied to himself, and the whole Book of Consolation (Isaiah 41-66) which holds such a great place in the Gospel. Chapter 61 invites the joy of consecration, the unction of the spirit received in Jesus Christ, the consecration from which the mission to preach the Gospel to the poor is derived.

Always recognizable as a carpenter, Jesus did not preach the Gospel to the poor from outside and from above, but identified himself with them, in the way of a servant (Isaiah 42, 49, 50, 52) who is simultaneously the people and Jesus.

Isaiah 42:1-4; Matt. 12:11-21. The servant, gentle and humble.

Isaiah 49; Luke 1:31-35; 2:31-32. The servant, hidden and universal, intimate love, from which follows the powerful word.

Isaiah 50:4-6; John 3:4. The servant, docile and strong.

Isaiah, 52:13; Matt. 8:17, 26, 62; 27:38-60. The servant, suffering and compassionate.

These Old Testament texts are illuminated in the New Testament.

Luke 1:48: Magnificat. Song of the first call to the apostolate, thanks of the apostle for the grace received, the thanks of the poor people who know that in Jesus Christ God will reverse the unjust, established order, send away the rich empty handed, put down the mighty from their seats, raise up the poor and feed the hungry.

Matt. 5-8; Luke 6:20-49. The Gospel word shows how the spirit of Jesus lives on in everyday life.

Matt. 10; Luke 9:57—10:22. The apostolic word gives instructions for the authentic apostolate.

Matt. 18; Mark 6. The communal word lays down how the apostles must live together.

John 13. The communion word makes their communal life more profound in love, and makes the apostles no longer servants but friends introduced into the secret of the eucharist and the spirit.

Acts. 1 : 8-11; Matt. 28 : 18-20; Mark 16 : 15-20; Luke 24 : 44-49; John 20 : 20-21; 21 : 15-18. The word of the spirit draws down on them that spirit which will send them to the ends of the earth, the spirit through which Jesus will always be with them.

All these texts must be read, re-read, understood, learned, digested and prayed over ceaselessly. It is on these texts that the Companions base their "review of life" and their apostolate.

The Companions will also like to meditate on :
Acts 2 : 42-47; 4 : 32-35.
Romans 8 : 14, 30.
I Cor. 13; II Cor. 4 : 6-11.
Gal. 3 : 1.
Eph. 3 : 14—4 : 12.
Phil. 2 : 1-11; 4 : 4-9.
Col. 4 : 2-6.
I Thess. 2 : 7-13; 5 : 12-23.
I Tim. 1 : 6—2 : 13.
Heb. 2 : 10-18; 5 : 1, 10; 12 : 1-12.
James 2 : 1-9; 2 : 14-16.
I Peter 1 : 10-13; 1 : 22-24; 2 : 4-12; 2 : 18-25; 3 : 8; 5 : 1-4.
II Peter 1 : 12-21; 3 : 12-13.
I John 1 : 1-4; 3 : 16-18; 4 (entire).
Apoc. 2 : 4 and 17; 3 : 20; 21 : 1-7; 21 : 22; 22 : 16, 17, 20.

IV. WAY OF LIFE AND CHIEF LOYALTIES

The way of life is that of Jesus of Nazareth, the carpenter, extended into the apostolic life, that of St Paul the apostle. In short, it is the way of life of the working people in whose country we find ourselves but with the obligations imposed by loyalty and love for Jesus Christ.

1. *External Way of Life*

The Companions live in working-class lodgings, rooms or tenements, and never in property of their own or in an ecclesiastical community.

They dress like poor workers, simply, and without seeking to out do the very poorest, but simply to be poor. Jesus was dressed like a simple carpenter of his day and his country.

They eat like the workers in whose midst they live, avoiding all excess that might endanger their health and reduce their working capacity.

They earn their living by manual or technical labour, labour as humble as that of Jesus or Paul, fitting into the type of society in which they live, and to its needs.

According to apostolic or practical necessity, the Companions live in small groups of two or three. Should a Companion live on his own, he must be sufficiently close to a group of two or three to be able to have daily contact with his fellow Companions.

For the rest, the Companions form an apostolic team of up to twelve members within the same geographical area, and come together at least once a fortnight to review their apostolate (Cf. Organization and Groups).

2. *Their Main Loyalties*

"And I will betroth you to me for ever; I will betroth you to me in righteousness, and in justice, in steadfast love and in mercy. I will betroth you to me in faithfulness: and you shall know the Lord" (Osee 2 : 19).

Faithfulness makes for knowledge: Jesus made this clear: "If a man loves me, he will keep my word and my Father will love him, and we will come to him, and make our home with him" (John 14 : 23).

(i) *Prayer*

Daily prayer. Three hours (cf. apostolic prayer): One hour of liturgy: mass, office, actual participation (or spiritual if actual participation is impossible) in the liturgical action of the Church for her bridegroom. The Companions draw sustenance from the divine liturgy.

One hour of Gospel or Bible reading. This reading will always be communion with Jesus, who is sought and loved through the texts. For the New Testament the Greek liturgical cycle can be followed. For the Old Testament the inspiration can be the Roman breviary. The whole Bible is to be read at least once a year; in any case the New Testament in its entirety, and the principal books of the Old Testament: Genesis, Exodus, Deuteronomy, Ruth, Samuel, Kings, and a general survey of biblical history up to Jesus: Job, the Psalms, the Canticles and the Prophets, and in particular Isaiah.

One hour of adoration in spirit and in truth before the Blessed Sacrament or in some solitary spot. We renew our faith in Jesus who is present by his Grace, our place in the Mystical Body of Christ, his personal love for us, and his saving love for all those to whom he has sent us. Contemplation of the Mystery of Jesus whose servants and witnesses we are.

Weekly Prayer. Confession (the examination of conscience can be made on one or other of the texts listed. . . . The Beatitudes. I Cor. 13 . . .) Choose a day, hold to it, and prepare for it in advance. Make confession an act of redeeming love (purification of the Church of which we are members, the bride purified by Jesus [Eph. 5:26]. An act of personal love: to be pardoned is to be loved [Cf. Osee]).

Monthly Prayer. A day of recollection, in solitude.

Annual Prayer. A week of real retreat, completely devoted to prayer and true silence.

Fraternal Prayer. As far as possible the Companions of the apostolate will pray together, by taking part in the liturgy together, by Bible readings, or by reviewing their life and apostolate together. . . . This review of their life and their apostolate is in effect prayer, a mutual seeking for the Saviour in our life and our apostolate. Every week a review of our life; every fortnight a review of our apostolate.

(ii) *Consecrated and Universal Love*

Intimacy and universality of the heart.

The consecration of the Companions of Jesus of Nazareth implies such an urgent love of Christ that it pre-supposes perfect chastity—that intimate love of the Christian who sacrifices physical love so that his love may blossom into a universal love.

This love is complete union with Jesus of Nazareth, consecration in him, the opening of our hearts to all those to whom he has sent us, whom we see and love in him; a redeeming sacrifice in a world which is a prey to sensual materialism; the proclamation of the good tidings of the resurrection and living witness to the resurrected one who draws us into his joy.

The Companions are completely at the disposal of the apostolate, which is lived in the thick of the world and demands a life of intense prayer, a fraternal spirit of mutual love within the group, a clarity and respect for human love, and a real sense of redeeming sacrifice.

(iii) *Fraternal Charity*

The love of Christ served and loved in his members.

Humble service to others in the group, to neighbours, or work-mates—as Jesus served the apostles, cooking for them, washing their feet. . . .

The Companions will take part in the working-class movement for social justice, joining the appropriate organizations, paying their subscriptions, supporting and encouraging everything calculated to improve conditions (such action must fit the circumstances, without assuming the responsibility for the temporal leadership).

Preaching the Gospel to the poor (cf. below, Apostolate) to welcome others and be at their disposal.

Solidarity with the common people.

(iv) *Work*

The Companions will work as all other working people do, whilst maintaining the intentions of the faith :

a) communion with Jesus the Carpenter living in the working people;

b) living in real poverty;

c) preaching the Gospel to the poor and ensuring the freedom of the Gospel;

d) completing in our bodies what is lacking in the Passion of Christ for his body, which is the Church; and

e) establishing the Church in the working world.

(v) *Poverty*

Real and material poverty such as that of poor working people. Social poverty : frequenting the common people. Spiritual poverty : of the heart, humility, forbearance (I Cor. 13).

(vi) *Obedience*

Obedience to Jesus of Nazareth; that is in practice :
a) to the essential loyalties (see above p. 130 ff.);

b) to the Church; to the episcopate, the leader of the apostolate;

c) to the group and the community as a cell of the Church and to those in positions of responsibility appointed by the episcopate (cf. below);

d) to work.

This obedience is simultaneously confidence, frankness with superiors and companions, exact information and knowledge of the position of the world in the mystery of Christ and His Church. It is always love even in the midst of the most painful sacrifice of personal will, or in the night of faith: "not my will but thine be done!"

(vii) *Study*

Particularly such as are indicated under Formation (see below p. 139 ff.).

One day a week; one week a year; and periodical sessions.

The Companions will keep themselves intellectually alive, humbly but resolutely, since this is a demand of truth and justice.

During the period of training, all available time is to be given to study.

V. ORGANIZATION AND GROUPS

The society receives its being and its mission from Christ through the episcopate. In practice it depends on the bishops who call the groups, on the Congregation of the Council in so far as it is a society of laymen consecrated for the apostolate and, as an apostolate under the Eastern Churches, on the Patriarchs and the Eastern Congregation. Thus it is completely dependent on the hierarchical Church and on the Apostolic See.

It is a matter for the episcopate to confirm the spirit that moves us, to give our society authority for its mission, to its members, to approve the election of members to the Committee of the community and to positions of responsibility, and to give them authority. The mission and the location of the groups are determined by the bishop in conjunction with the Committee or whoever is responsible for it.

The members of the community already consecrated by the bishop elect "the Committee" of the community. This Committee consists of a minimum of five members. It is elected for one year, and meets at least once during that year under the auspices of the bishop who represents all the bishops who have called the groups. It appoints one member to take responsibility for the community. It appoints those responsible for the communities and apostolic groups and assigns each member his place in conjunction with the bishop of the area. The Committee entrusts its appointed leader with the duty of keeping a constant eye on the progress of the community. The episcopate ratifies these decisions by its approval. All elections or appointments receive authority from the episcopate, which approves and grants mandate or jurisdiction. Authority does not proceed from the group itself but from the hierarchy, and this is what gives the members' obedience its Gospel value: "He who hears you, hears me." "How can men preach unless they are sent?"

Those who have responsibility in the community, the fraternity and the group bear the name of "servant", both in spirit and in fact (Luke 22:24-27; John 13:13-15; I Peter 5:3) and they behave accordingly. The servants of the fraternity or group of this or that region meet together according to local needs.

The group or fraternity is the expression and sign of charity, the vital organ of the apostolate. Charity, in fact, is giving, it is mutual support, the sign of Christ which more than anything else is brotherly love within the community: "By this all men will know that you are my disciples, if you have love for one another" (John 13:35).

The group, with its servant mandated by the bishop, has authority over its members, who owe it obedience. It is the organ midway between the members and the episcopate. It is the cell of the community and the Church. It takes its place in the life of the local church and of the local human community in which it lives. The group designates the places where its members live and work, and promotes the spirit of the apostolate.

There are three types of groups: the fraternal group which lives together, the apostolic group, and the training group. In any particular sector these are not separate but they are distinct.

The fraternal group consists of two or three members who live together, either in the same lodging or quite close to one another, meeting at least once a day for a meal, praying together daily and talking together about their life and about Christ Jesus. Once a week the fraternity meets to review its life. It is a centre of friendship and evangelical light.

The apostolic group embraces up to a dozen Companions (who work together for the Gospel in the same geographical or sociological sector). Every fortnight the members meet for prayer and study and to review their apostolic activity. Periodically the group will invite the bishop to visit them, or they will visit him, in order to inform him of their activities and to receive his instructions.

The training group is a fraternity consisting of one member already consecrated and acting as a servant to train and form one or two apprentice novices (I Thess. 2: 7-12). The Committee will also appoint one or two servants to be in charge of the training centres to which the training groups are attached (cf. Formation, p. 139 ff. below).

The fraternities and groups live in the spirit and manner of Christ's life with his apostles, and according to the behests he himself has given us: Matt. 18—in humility, prudence and respect; taking care not to lose even a single sheep; in fraternal correction, communal prayer, and ceaseless forgiveness, John 13-17. The simplest possible service, a personal sense of mystery, fraternal love in Christ, living in the world but not of the world, living in the spirit whilst awaiting its return, and sacerdotal prayer. Re-read in groups and fraternities the texts quoted under the heading "What manner of spirit are you of?" (p. 127 above). Thus the Companions of Nazareth live together with openness and mutual acceptance, in clarity, confidence and simplicity, in peace and gentleness, with respect for each other's personality.

They faithfully attend all meetings and gatherings, and prepare for them in advance, knowing that they each bear the burden of all, and that all bear the burden of each.

The review of life takes place at a meeting of the fraternity, in the name of Jesus, who is always amongst us (Matt. 18:10); we examine our life or apostolate in the light of the Gospel, in order to analyse it and redirect it. The revision consists in recapitulating the main points of our essential loyalties sketched above. This or that text, in which Jesus explains the spirit we should have, is read. News and information are also exchanged and discussed at these meetings.

In reviewing their apostolate, the Companions working in a particular sector pool the facts of their working life, of the life of working people, of the apostolate and of the Church, mutually rectifying their judgements, and co-ordinating their apostolate in the life of the whole local church. At these meetings the servant, or, better still, the Bishop himself whenever he can be present, will always have the last word, which all will accept with gratitude, as an expression of Jesus in our midst (I Thess. 5:12-28).

VI. FORMATION

Before sending them out on their mission, Jesus trained his apostles for three years, inviting them to "come and see", having them live with him, taking them to one side to explain to them in detail the nature of his thought, and step by step calling them, naming them, consecrating them, and finally sending them out on their mission.

In the same way those who wish to become "Companions of Nazareth" are first invited to "come and see" (John 1:39). At the end of a year the apprentice-novice is called by the Bishop (Mark 1:17). In the following year he is named (Luke 6:13). One year later he is consecrated (John 15:16—17:19). And finally in the fifth year he is sent (Matt. 28:18-20). These periods are not inflexible, and in any particular instance they may be shortened by the Committee.

At the end of these five years the apprentice apostle should be thoroughly formed and trained morally, spiritually and intellectually.

a) During his *moral training* in the first two years, that is to say, before he is "named", the apprentice-novice is given no mission or responsibility. He makes himself completely available, he is receptive, obedient and docile both at work, amongst the working people, and in the fraternity. He lives at Nazareth in silence. Each week he requests the fraternity, or at least the servant (i.e. the one responsible, see above p. 137), to point out and correct his errors. After his nomination he may be given certain responsibilities, and it will be his duty to vote for the Committee. During this apprenticeship-novitiate the apprentice-novice will learn a trade, and at the same time will train himself in prayer and the main loyalties. Throughout, the Companion is trained morally for the life of the fraternity and the group apostolate, living the essential loyalties of the apostle (cf above p. 130 f.).

b) His *spiritual training* is based on the Bible, the liturgy and the life of the Church itself. In reading the Bible, and above all the Gospels (cf. Prayer) under the direction of the servant or the person responsible, the apprentice-novice lets himself be formed by the spirit of Christ, as Peter, Andrew and John let themselves be formed by Jesus with the same realism and the same determination. Where this Bible reading is concerned it is a good thing to follow the liturgical cycle. The Church bears us in prayer in the liturgy and unites us to Christ. The liturgy educates us on condition that we really and actively live the liturgical act. There is a time for prayer and for liturgy. The one educates us for the other. Ultimately it is the whole life of the Church that shapes and forms us through her saints, who have lived this life and who are still living with us in Christ, and who have left us their writings and their lives, in her various Eastern and Western communities, and in her actual presence in the world. By living according to the rhythm of the Church we follow in her path as the child at home follows in the path of its mother.

c) His *intellectual training* embraces :

The study of the Bible : summary chronology, the order of the different books, a more profound knowledge of the books and the texts listed above. He should study the text of the Bible, and if possible Hebrew also as a living language or Greek.

The study of the Church in her mystery, her history (from the stand-point of the missionary apostolic Church), and her structure in order through faith to see Christ in his Church, to discern the two without ever dissociating the human and the divine, and to appreciate the Church in all her plenitude, in her catholicity and her apostolicity. The missionary encyclicals and those on the Eastern Church are studied. And finally, the separated churches are studied in an ecumenical spirit in their relationship to the Catholic Church.

The social doctrines of the Church as laid down in encyclicals since Leo XIII, and in the utterances of the great Christian thinkers from the days of the Fathers of the Early Church to our own day.

The analysis of great social systems (marxism).

The study of the great non-Christian religions: Judaism and the mystery of Israel, Islam, Hinduism, Buddhism....

It is during the course of the five years between his application and his sending forth that the apprentice-novice receives his training. He is also given a year of his novitiate in which to absorb the Bible in prayer, living on what he has saved the previous year, and acquiring a personal knowledge of Jesus.

These training centres are organized as far as possible in biblical neighbourhoods: Nazareth, Genesareth and Jerusalem. The apprentice-novices are organized in their training groups around these centres. Some of the Companions will extend their studies to other parts, in particular Rome and Jerusalem. Those who are called to the priesthood take the normal courses, but must have been ordained previously and have received their apostolic training. Those who enter the community as fully ordained priests will receive the same apostolic training, thus renewing their acquaintance under a new light, more simple and more real, with what they have already studied and experienced. After their period of training, which can vary from case to case, all that remains is for them to receive the apostolate from the hands of the Bishop (cf. below p. 143 f.).

VII. STAGES

These years of training are divided into stages by the application, the invitation, the call, the nomination, the consecration and the apostolate, in accordance with the rhythm adopted by Jesus with his disciples. This rhythm encourages an increasing participation in the life of the Church, and a growing intimacy with Jesus of Nazareth. Should the servants be doubtful this time of waiting may be extended. At each stage there is a particular grace marked by a gesture. There may be no more than three months between the candidate's application and the invitation, and in this time the candidate will live our life in a fraternity, but without taking part in the periodical reviews of life and apostolate.

The Invitation

The invitation to the candidate is very simple, like the "come and see" addressed by Jesus to Andrew and John (John 1 : 39). The servant of the fraternity or group to which the candidate has made his application conveys the answer to him by saying "come and see", and in this way he introduces him into a revision meeting of the group.

The Call

At the end of a year—if the fraternity and the group regard him as suitable—the apprentice-novice is presented to the Bishop, who calls him by saying: "Come I will make you a fisher of men." For this purpose, however, the Bishop may delegate a priest.

The Nomination

At the end of this second year—if he is judged suitable by the fraternity and the group—he is again presented to the Bishop, who will give him his apostolic name (whereby his baptismal name may be changed or left as it is), for example: "Andrew, you will henceforth be called Isaiah, and I name you a Companion of Jesus of Nazareth, the Carpenter." Or if there is to be no change of name: "Andrew, I name you a Companion of Jesus of Nazareth, the Carpenter" (Luke 6 : 12-16).

The Consecration

At the end of the third year, and if the judgement of the group, the fraternity and the Committee of the Community is favourable, the Companion is once more presented to the Bishop to be consecrated. The Bishop lays on his hands and pronounces the words of Jesus reading from Isaiah in the synagogue of Nazareth (Luke 4; Isaiah 61).

The Bishop gives the Companion an ikon or crucifix, saying: "Before your eyes Jesus Christ was publicly portrayed as crucified" (Gal. 3 : 1). "No longer do I call you servant, but friend" (John 15 : 15). "The friend of the bridegroom, who stands and hears him, rejoices greatly at the bridegroom's voice; therefore this joy of mine is now full. He must increase, but I must decrease" (John 3 : 29-30). "Sanctify them in the truth; thy word is truth. . . . And for their sake I consecrate myself, that they also may be consecrated in truth" (John 17 : 17, 19).

The Bishop annoints the Companion's hands with paschal oil, saying: "Is this not the Carpenter? I consecrate you with the hands of the Carpenter."

The Apostolate

At the end of the fifth year the consecrated Companion is presented by the Community to the Bishop in order that he may be sent out to preach the Gospel. The Bishop says "the sacerdotal prayer" (John 17). He presents the Companion with a Bible, saying: "Peace be with you: as the Father has sent me, even so I send you. You shall be my witnesses in Jerusalem, and in all Judea and Samaria, and to the end of the earth. Go therefore and make disciples of all nations . . . teaching them to observe all that I have commanded you; and lo, I am with you always, to the close of the age. And when I go and prepare a place for you, I will come again, and will take you to myself."[1] The Bishop then gives the Companion the kiss of peace.

These various stages lead neither to the religious life nor to the priesthood. Their only end is consecration to Jesus of Nazareth for the preaching of the Gospel to the poor in the society of the Companions of Nazareth.

If the Companions are called to the priesthood they receive the normal ordination, after their consecration to preach the Gospel to the poor, and with the approval of their Bishop they remain as priests in that community. The problem of integration will have to be examined in the spirit of the Mission de France. If a priest wishes to enter into the community he must, after a suitable period of formation, be sent to preach the Gospel to the poor (the final state).

VIII. THE APOSTOLATE

The apostolate is not action, and still less activism. Neither is it a mixed life (contemplation-activity). It is not a question of doing an apostolate, but of being an apostle by participating in the apostolate of Jesus, who was sent by his Father, and extending his mission in the Church through the episcopate.

The apostolate is prayer and preaching, the intimacy of love blossoming into universal love, contemplation of the

[1] John 20:21; Acts 1:8; Matt. 28:20; John 14:3.

mystery of Jesus and revelation of the mystery. The Companions are assiduous in prayer and in the ministry of the Word (Acts. 6:4).

Prayer is an apostolate in itself, but it must be apostolic. It is prayer that saves the world, bringing it back to the fidelity of love. "You must dwell as mine for many days" (Osee 3:3). "And for their sakes I consecrate myself, that they also may be consecrated in truth. I do not pray for these only, but also for those who believe in me through their word" (John 17:19-20). At the same time prayer, like perfect chastity, is a witness to the existence of another love in the midst of a world without God and without love. And finally it is the source of the Word. To be well adapted to a working life, to the life of the poor and of working people, prayer must be properly directed.

The Word is not our word. In the Church it is Jesus himself; it is he who speaks, as it is he who prays in his Church. We are caught up in this prayer and in this Word. The living Word gives life. The creative Word is made flesh and dwells in his Church. It is the work of the spirit in the Church, like the incarnation in Mary. Through it the Church bears humanity in grace to Christ. Through it, new cells of the Church are formed since the faith is communicated by its means.

The Companions are called to spread the Gospel. They announce the Good Tidings to those who have not yet heard them, to the poor who, alas! are still neglected to the profit of the rich even in the Church, to people outside the Church, to the de-christianized masses, to our separated brethren. "It goes hard with me if I do not preach the Gospel."

The Word is first of all the silent announcement of the Gospel by means of a life truly and visibly in accordance with the Gospel (cf. above, Way of Life (p. 130 f.) and Main Loyalties (p. 131 ff.)). But it is also the word in the proper sense of the term. It is not enough to announce the word of the Gospel in silence. The Gospel must be shouted from the house tops. The Companions are always ready to give an answer to every man who questions them about the hope that is in them (I Peter 3:15) and they are always ready to announce Christ as the secret of love revealed to his friends. Here the word presupposes a double love: love for Christ and love for the brother to whom Christ is announced.

The Gospel is preached by the word through casual conversation, conferences, writing, radio, films—in every way open to the Companions, provided always that they remain poor, live a working life and avoid all proselytism.

The word, like prayer, expresses itself also in definite social action, which is the sign of charity, without the Companions being involved in the management of temporal organizations or works. However, the Companions take part in the working-class movement for social justice and for the advancement of the poor to greater material well being. According to circumstances they encourage already existing movements, or bring into being whatever a real and practical love for Jesus living in his members requires. Living as the poor live, or preaching the Gospel, does not satisfy them; they always remember that Jesus said: "I was hungry, I was naked, I was homeless. . . ." So he still is, and the poor will always be with us. It is not enough to love them by turning towards them with condescension or by sharing their poverty. With the sword of the word we must act in season and out of season to see that Jesus in his suffering and overworked members is fed, clothed and lodged. . . .

Thus the Companions take part in the rise of people and of under-developed countries towards a more human and just state. At the same time they exhort the rich and the developed countries, by pointing out to them how far they are removed from the Gospel if they do not bother their heads about the poor man at their gate.

Within the Church herself and outside the Church the Companions work with all their strength for the union of all Christians in the one true Church, taking an active part in the ecumenical movement in order to abolish the scandal of divided Christendom, and to let the glory of the Mystical Body of Christ shine in all its glorious unity.

This whole apostolate presupposes a profound oneness with the Church and therefore the Companions, both personally and as a body, work in close harmony with the whole of the local Church, the bishop and the parish, and the lay apostolate. They are in union with all spiritual and religious branches, and most particularly with contemplatives and with worker-apostolate movements. By their word and their love they contribute to the perfect fidelity of the whole Church to her bridegroom, Jesus of Nazareth, the Carpenter.

FOR THE WOMEN COMPANIONS OF THE CARPENTER

For women, the Companions' Way of Life is by and large the same, though there are certain differences, particularly where the Stages (VII) and the Apostolate (VIII) are concerned:

VII. The Stages

The *invitation* is the same as for the male Companions.

The call: The apprentice-novice is presented to the Bishop who calls upon her (the Bishop may delegate this to a priest), saying: "The Holy Spirit will come upon you" (Luke 1:35). Then he places a ring upon the finger of her right hand, saying: "The Lord hath said: 'I will betroth you to me in righteousness, and in justice, in steadfast love and in mercy' " (Osee 2:19).

The nomination: at the end of this second year, after a favourable judgement on the part of the group and the fraternity, the one called is again presented to the Bishop, who gives her her apostolic name (which may, or may not, be the same as her baptismal name); for example: "Joan, henceforth you will be called Miriam, and I name you a Companion of Jesus of Nazareth, the Carpenter" (Luke 6: 12-16).

The consecration: at the end of the third year, after a favourable judgement on the part of the group, the fraternity, and the Committee of the community, the Companion is presented to the Bishop to be consecrated. The Bishop lays on his hands and pronounces the words Jesus read from Isaiah in the synagogue of Nazareth (Luke 4; Isaiah 61).

He then places the ring on her left hand, saying: "The Lord hath said: 'I will betroth you to me in faithfulness; and you shall know the Lord' " (Osee 2:20).

The Bishop then anoints her hands with the paschal oil saying: "Is this not the Carpenter? I consecrate you with the hands of the Carpenter."

The apostolate: at the end of the fifth year the consecrated Companion is presented to the Bishop by the community in order that she may be sent forth to preach the Gospel. The Bishop says the sacerdotal prayer (John 17). He then presents her with a Bible, saying: "Peace be with you: as the Father has sent me, even so I send you. You shall be my witnesses in Jerusalem, and in all Judea, and Samaria, and to the end of the earth. Go therefore and make disciples of all nations ... teaching them to observe all I have commanded you; and lo, I am with you always, to the close of the age. And when I go and prepare a place for you, I will come again and will take you to myself."[1]

The Bishop then reads the Gospel of St John, Chapter 20, verses 11-18. The one who is sent forth now kisses the Bishop's hand.

VIII. *The Apostolate*

The ceremony is the same as for the male companions (cf. above), with the added observation: "All your apostolic life you will preserve the discretion proper to consecrated women."

"They mingle with the apostles and disciples, with Mary and the Holy Women, at the same time preserving in their hearts the attitude of Mary of Bethany as a sign of interior grace, in the condition of a woman who awaits the return of her husband, with the obedience of Mary Magdalene: 'Do not hold me but go to my brethren and tell them. . . .' And finally they see in the Virgin of Cana, attentive to God and men, the heart of all prayer, the mystery of the word incarnate."

GLORY TO THEE, LORD!

Approved and blessed
GEORGE HAKIM
On the Nativity of Mary, 8 September 1962.

---

[1] John 20:21; Acts 1:8; Matt. 28:20; John 14:3.

APPENDIX II

EXTRACTS FROM CARDINAL LERCARO'S DECLARATION AT THE FIRST SESSION OF THE VATICAN COUNCIL

Appendix II

Extracts from Cardinal Lercaro's Declaration at the First Session of the Vatican Council

Venerable brothers,

My intention is to make us more attentive to that (visible) aspect of the Mystery of Christ in the Church which is not only permanent and essential, but of the greatest historical topicality.

I mean that the Mystery of Christ in the Church is always, but particularly today, the Mystery of Christ in the poor, since the Church, as our Holy Father Pope John XXIII has said, is truly the Church of all, but is particularly "the Church of the poor"....

None of the schemata which have been put before us, or which are to be put before us, seem to take this essential and primordial aspect of the Mystery of Christ into account in any explicit and formal project which accords with historic circumstances.

Poverty was foretold by the prophets as the authentic sign of the messianic consecration of Christ.

It was exalted by the Mother of the Saviour herself in the incarnation of the Word.

It was made manifest by the birth, the childhood, the private life and the public ministry of Jesus.

It is the law and foundation of the kingdom of God.

Its mark is stamped on all the effusions of grace and on the life of the Church from the days of the apostolic community to those periods of the Church's most intense interior renewal and exterior expansion.

Finally, it will be sanctioned for all eternity by reward or punishment at the second and glorious coming of the Son of God at the end of time. . . .

We shall not be doing our task sufficiently well, and our spirit will not be sufficiently responsive to God's design and man's expectation unless, we place the Mystery of Christ in the poor and the preaching of the Gospel to the poor at the heart and centre of our doctrinal and legislative work at this Council.

This, in fact, is an obvious, practical, topical and urgent task for our day.

Certainly by comparison with other epochs, it seems that in our day the poor have the Gospel less preached to them, their hearts seem farther away from and foreign to the Mystery of Christ in the Church.

At the same time ours is an epoch in which, by agonising and almost dramatic questions, the spirit of man turns to and closely examines the mystery of poverty and the condition of the poor, both the condition of the individual and that of whole peoples who live in destitution, and yet are newly becoming conscious of their proper rights.

This is an epoch in which the poverty of the majority (two-thirds) of mankind is outraged by the immense riches of a minority, in which poverty inspires a greater horror amongst the masses every day, and in which the worldly man is plagued by the thirst for riches.

In recalling, as others have already done, the problem of winning the poor for the Gospel, I am far from wishing to add another subject to the list, already very long, of the subjects to be treated by the Council. However, I do wish to affirm:

If we treat this subject of winning the poor for the Gospel as just another one of the many themes which must occupy the attention of the Council we shall not satisfy the most real and most profound exigencies of our day (including our great hope of furthering the unity of all Christendom)— indeed, we shall make it impossible for us to do so.

If, as has been said many times, the Church herself is in truth the theme of the Council, then in full accord with the eternal truth of the Gospel, and at the same time in full and perfect accord with the present world we can only affirm that the subject of the Council is most certainly the Church, particularly because she is above all "the Church of the poor".... I would like to make the following proposals:

In its future deliberations, let the Council give not merely some attention, but pride of place, so to speak, to the development of the Gospel doctrine of the holy poverty of Christ in the Church. In particular, it should clarify God's design in choosing poverty as the sign and form of the presence and saving grace of the Word made flesh amongst men (and this sacrament is great, let me say, in Christ and in the Church).

May equal priority be given to the development of the evangelical doctrine of the eminent dignity of the poor as privileged members of the Church, since the Word of God has chosen to hide his glory in these members until the end of time....

In all the subjects the Council will deal with, may the ontological connection between the presence of Christ in the poor, and the two other profound realities of the Mystery of Christ in the Church, namely the presence of Christ in the eucharistic action by means of which the Church is made one and is constituted, and the presence of Christ in the sacred hierarchy which instructs and governs the Church, be brought out and clarified....

Again, may due emphasis be given to the historical connection between our sincere and active recognition of the eminent dignity of the poor in the kingdom of God and the Church on the one hand and the obstacles we are able to see, on the other hand, to a readjustment of our ecclesiastical institutions and the ways and means of achieving this.

This having been said, it will suffice as a kind of conclusion and practical confirmation to give a few examples of the subjects in which it will be necessary to pursue our decrees for reform—with wisdom and moderation, of course, but also without timidity or compromise:

1. A definition of the ways in which the material resources of the Church may be used, and in particular those whose outward appearance seems to conform less with the holy poverty of the Church, in accordance with the words: "Gold and silver have I none, but what I have I give you."

2. The drafting of a new style or "etiquette" for the Supreme Pontiff, one which will not shock the sensibilities of our contemporaries or give the poor occasion for scandal, lest we who very often really are poor should outwardly appear to be rich.

3. Fidelity to holy poverty, not only individually but also collectively, on the part of our religious bodies.

4. A new attitude in the economic sphere, together with the abandonment of certain institutions which belong to the past, which are no longer of use today and which represent obstacles to our free and generous apostolic work.

If we show ourselves obedient to the plan of Divine Providence, affirming and proclaiming the primacy of winning the poor for the Gospel, it will not be difficult, with the aid of the Holy Spirit and the protection of Mary, Mother of God, to find a valid method for all our problems, whether doctrinal or practical to present in its entirety the eternal and immutable Gospel of God; and at the same time to present it in such a way that it will be easier to unite the whole Christian family, so that the Father and Christ may be one and all hearts may be more deeply touched, and the hopes of all men fulfilled in our day—in particular, the hopes of the poor in the Church of Christ, who, being rich, made himself poor in order that we might all become rich in his grace and glory.